RYUHO OKAWA

LOVE FOR THE FUTURE

BUILDING ONE WORLD OF FREEDOM AND DEMOCRACY UNDER GOD'S TRUTH

IRH PRESS

BOOKS
IRH PRESS
New York

ISBN 13: 978-1-942125-60-0
ISBN 10: 1-942125-60-7

Printed in Canada

First Edition

Cover © Shutterstock/Neo Edmund
/alwaysloved afilm

Contents

PART I: LECTURE

CHAPTER ONE
Love for the Future

CHAPTER TWO
The Fact and the Truth

CHAPTER THREE
Love Beyond Hatred

FURTHER READING
What is True Democracy?

Excerpt from "The Realization of Buddhaland Utopia"

❧ PART II: SPIRITUAL INTERVIEW ❧

CHAPTER FOUR
Spiritual Interview with the Guardian Spirit of Xi Jinping (Excerpt)

CHAPTER FIVE
Spiritual Interview with the Guardian Spirit of Vladimir Putin (Excerpt)

CHAPTER SIX
Spiritual Interview with the Guardian Spirit of Angela Merkel (Excerpt)

CHAPTER SEVEN

Spiritual Interviews with the Guardian Spirit of Donald Trump (Excerpts)

There are two parts to this book. Part I is a compilation of 3 lectures and Q & A sessions from Okawa's visits around the world, in a verbatim style. Part II is a compilation of spiritual interviews that Okawa held using his spiritual ability.

Chapters 1, 2, 6, and 7 were originally recorded in English, and Chapters 3, 4, and 5 are English translations of recordings done in Japanese.

For details on spiritual interviews, see the section, "What is a Spiritual Message?" in the end pages of this book.

PART I

LECTURE

Chapter ONE

Love for the Future

Lecture given on October 7, 2018
at The Ritz-Carlton
Berlin, Germany

PREFACE

More than a month has passed since I gave this lecture in Germany. It feels like I was dreaming.

The content of the lecture is clear and logical. Many of the German audience commented that my lecture was bold and courageous. They were astonished and moved, saying "We can't believe there is a Japanese religious leader who can give such a lecture here in Germany." As for me, I strongly wished for our dear German brothers, who could not even raise their right hand to ask a question or cross their arms in front of them because it reminds them of Hitler, to wake up from their nightmare soon and become people who think about the future and act positively.

I hope from the bottom of my heart that this giant bullet shot during the final years of the Merkel administration will bear fruits, for the future of the EU and the future of the world, as the love from God.

Ryuho Okawa
Master & CEO of Happy Science Group
Nov. 16, 2018

From the Preface given for the book, Mirai e no Ai [*Love for the Future*] (Tokyo: IRH Press, 2018).

1

My Impression of Germany
And the Message from
Emperor Showa in My Dream

Danke. Danke schön. Guten Tag. Ich heisse Ryuho Okawa. Ich komme aus Japan ("Thank you. Thank you very much. Hello. My name is Ryuho Okawa. I came from Japan" in German). From now on, I speak English. OK? [*Audience laughs.*]

"Love for the Future" is today's theme. But firstly, I will speak my impression I felt in these three or four days in Berlin. This is a beautiful city, I felt so. But something is lacking, I felt also. I think and think and think, *denken* ("think" in German) and denken and denken about that. One thing is, you are too much eco-oriented. It means you lack electricity, I felt so.* In Tokyo, we use more electricity, so maybe Chancellor Angela Merkel has a very powerful idea of saving money, I guess so. But it's not all my impression.

Another one is some sadness I felt. When I stayed here, on the first night, of course my hotel is near here and near Potsdamer Platz, I had a dream of Emperor Showa Hirohito†, three times that night.

---

* In Germany, people tend to save electricity in order to deal with the rising electricity costs caused by nuclear power phase-out.

† Hirohito (1901–1989) was the 124th Emperor of Japan who reigned from 1926 until his death in 1989. He is now referred to primarily by his posthumous name, Emperor Showa. The word Showa is the name of the era coinciding with the Emperor's reign.

He told me something. This is Berlin and as you know, the Potsdam Declaration‡ was done near here and then the post-war political regime was established, so Emperor Hirohito asked me, instead of him, "Please say hello to the German people and if possible, make them happier." He said so. It's a political problem, but firstly, I'll say about that. Emperor Hirohito was the emperor during the Second World War, so more than half of the German people think of him as someone like Adolf Hitler, but indeed he is not.

I wrote about another world in *The Laws of the Sun* [see Figure 1]. Here, we are living in the third dimensional world [see Figure 2], but when we leave this world, we enter into the fourth dimensional world. Here, this fourth dimensional world, we have a heavenly part and a hellish part. People who lived, in a nutshell, badly go to hell and who generally lived good go to heaven. This is the first step. Then, next step is the fifth dimensional world. This is the world of good people like you, as you think you are, or more than that, you are. Good people are living in the next dimension. And the sixth dimensional world is the world of people who are near "small god"-like people. For example, great politicians, scholars, or other great people who made a lot of influence on the people of the world. This is the sixth dimensional world.

---

‡ The Potsdam Declaration stated Japan's terms of surrender in World War II. It was issued by the U.S., the U.K., and the Republic of China on July 26, 1945 in Potsdam, a city near Berlin. Japan accepted the declaration, which led to the end of the war.

I mentioned about Emperor Hirohito. He is living in this sixth dimensional world now, but the lower part of the sixth dimensional world. He, himself was one of the national gods of Japan, so when he was born, he might have come from the upper side of the sixth dimensional world. But through the Second World War and by living 40 years after it and making the Japanese economic prosperity, what he did was a little bad and a little good, so totally, he was judged as the lower part of the sixth dimensional world.

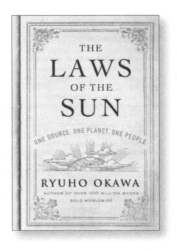

Figure 1.
The Laws of the Sun
(New York: IRH Press, 2018)

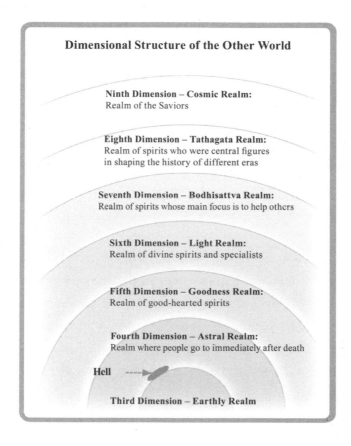

Dimensional Structure of the Other World

Ninth Dimension – Cosmic Realm:
Realm of the Saviors

Eighth Dimension – Tathagata Realm:
Realm of spirits who were central figures
in shaping the history of different eras

Seventh Dimension – Bodhisattva Realm:
Realm of spirits whose main focus is to help others

Sixth Dimension – Light Realm:
Realm of divine spirits and specialists

Fifth Dimension – Goodness Realm:
Realm of good-hearted spirits

Fourth Dimension – Astral Realm:
Realm where people go to immediately after death

Hell

Third Dimension – Earthly Realm

Figure 2.
The other world is divided into different realms from the fourth dimensional
Astral Realm to the ninth dimensional Cosmic Realm. Each spirit lives in the
realm that corresponds to his or her level of faith and state of mind. Hell is just a
small portion of the fourth dimension.

2

The Status Quo of The Spirit of Hitler and The Purification of Europe

Then, next you want to hear about Adolf Hitler. This might be the hidden part of Germany, but I'm a foreigner and I don't know about Germany a lot. I will say something, but it's a foreigner's opinion, so please hear about that not so seriously. It's just my impression and just my opinion. Not all of the Japanese people think so, but I just think so.

I already published the spiritual message from Führer Adolf Hitler.* He became warmer and warmer recently because we Happy Science worked a lot and he can rely on the new movement in the spiritual meaning. It means we opened the German branch temple and dispatched a lot of books in German, French and other languages, so there occurred purifying of Europe in these 30 years and their sin is becoming lighter and lighter, year by year.

---

* The author recorded spiritual interviews with Hitler on June 2, 2010 and March 25, 2016. See *Kokka Shakaishugi towa nani ka* (lit. "What is National Socialism?") (Tokyo: IRH Press, 2010) and *Hitler teki Shiten kara Kensho suru Sekai de Mottomo Kiken na Dokusaisha no Miwake kata* (lit. "Investigating from Hitler's Perspective: How to Identify the World's Most Dangerous Dictator") (Tokyo: IRH Press, 2016).

So, he is not so great a demon nowadays.[†] He is waiting for your new activities. This is a very difficult theme, but I want to say about this firstly.

3
The 20th Century:
A Century of War and Racial Hatred

Hitler got his legitimacy in 1933 and established anti-Semitism laws, or anti-Jewish laws, in 1935, but at that time, he studied a lot from the United States of America. In the United States of America, there were also discrimination laws, for example, discrimination against the Native American Indians. There were several million Native American Indians, but White Americans killed a lot of Native Americans, so at that time, there was only one-tenth of Native American Indians left. At the same time, there was discrimination regarding African Americans. At that time, they were called "Negroes." When we study history, at the age of Abraham Lincoln, the black people had been emancipated, we usually think

---

[†] Spirits in hell who actively commit evil are called "demons" or "devils." Hitler is still going through the process of self-reflection in hell, but even a devil like him could reform and revert to an ordinary hellish spirit. Should they improve further and people's grudge toward them weaken, they could escape from hell.

like that. But after the assassination of Abraham Lincoln, 100 years had passed and at that time, there was discrimination against black people and also yellow people including the Chinese, Koreans, and Japanese. So, Martin Luther King, Jr. fought against discrimination in the 1960s. That's the truth.

So, the Second World War had a great connection with racism. After this war, there occurred the independence of India from the United Kingdom, and other countries of Asia from colonization. As you know, Nelson Mandela of South Africa became the president of that country in 1994. At that time, a black person became the president. Next, as you know, President Barack Obama became so in the United States.

So, the 20th century was a century of war, but in another meaning, it was a century of hatred of races. We must learn a lot about that. I said the anti-Semitism laws, or anti-Jewish laws, were established in Germany in 1935, which were called the Nuremberg Laws. They were very much influenced by the United States law. Adolf Hitler also admired Franklin Roosevelt. He did the New Deal policy. It's Keynesian economics. He led the Tennessee Valley Authority plan. Hitler praised Roosevelt a lot and was influenced by him a lot. Germany recovered from the recession that came from the ruin of the First World War. After that, he did too much and killed a lot of Jewish people. It's true, it's a sin. He cannot escape from that conclusion. But at that age, the 20th century, people of the world were thinking about what is racism, what is good and evil, what comes from God, and what comes from Hell, so this was a very important experience and we paid a lot of cost about that. Here, in Europe, more than 50 million people were killed. It's a sadness. Germany lost twice; the First World War and the Second World War.

4
The Most Important Thing is "Love for the Future"

Now, the age, situation, and societies are changing. The EU started and at the first stage of the EU, Germany was the center of economy of the EU. They, the people of Europe and the people of the world, thought like that. The second stage began in 2003. It's the starting year of the Iraq War. Next was the 2008 Lehman Brothers collapse, the Great Recession. Around this time, Germany changed into another appearance, I mean, Germany came to have political influence on, of course, all the EU and other countries. Not only the economy, but also the politics. So, you are in the process of changing Germany.

But the most important thing is today's theme, "Love for the Future." It's regarding the future. You lost twice, but next, you'll never fail again. The Third World War will occur around the South China Sea between 2025 and 2050. The United States and Japan are preparing for that. Xi Jinping has dictatorship in Beijing and he, himself, appeared like Adolf Hitler's Nazism, Italian Fascism, or Soviet Union Stalinism-like movement. We are near China, so we're looking at China and we can foresee the future. For example, China, after the Second World War, invaded Tibet, the Buddhist country. Next was Uyghur; they were conquered and occupied, and then Mongolia were. Now, they are changing Hong Kong. Hong Kong was promised to continue its freedom system for 50 years, but within 20 years, they are suppressed by Beijing. Now, they experienced the Umbrella Revolution* already. The Umbrella Revolution, only three or four years before that, I made a lecture in Hong Kong† and said to them, "You should choose the third way." They were thinking just to escape from China or just to be included in China, but I indicated that, "You should have enough influence on Beijing. Beijing should be changed like Hong Kong and Taiwan."

Beijing must never conduct like Fascism, Nazism, or Stalinism-like countries. It's going on, but someone must stop that. For example, China is very far from here, Germany. Regarding your foreign trade amount, number one is China. It's too far from you, but around China, I mean Taiwan, Vietnam, the Philippines, Thailand, Myanmar, Sri Lanka, and Nepal, these countries are under the shadow of a gigantic empire. It's imperialism and more-

---

* The Umbrella Revolution was a democratization movement that occurred in Hong Kong in 2014. Students participated in a large-scale protest calling for a freer election after the Chinese government tried to screen candidates for the election of the chief executive of Hong Kong. The movement got its name after people used umbrellas to resist against pepper spray used by the police.

† See Chapter 2.

than-imperialism, it's totalitarianism. They are fearing about that. So, sometimes, for example, the Philippines or Vietnam, they asked Japan, "Please provide us patrolling ships, 10 or more than that." It's a very dangerous situation. China has missiles in the South China Sea area. Even the United States Seventh Fleet is included in their missile attack plan from inside of China. Japan is now researching the next defensive missile with the speed of Mach 5 or faster to protect United States aircraft inside of Chinese missile range. This is the reality.

5
Teach China about Freedom, Democracy, and Faith

So, I just want to say that Chancellor Merkel earned a lot from China, I know. Of course, I know. It's of course good for the refugees from Africa and the Middle East. It's OK, of course. But if you choose one country, for example, Russia or China, it will change the future of human beings. What if you choose China and you obey the One Belt, One Road strategy of Xi Jinping, the Maritime Silk Road system? China lends a lot of money to the countries of the road, but if they, for example, Sri Lanka or another Middle East country, cannot pay back the money lent, China occupies that country. That is their thinking. The final aim is to control Germany. If they can control Germany, they can control the EU. This is their final strategy. So, please be wise about that. The opinion of German people is that they dislike Putin's Russia, I hear like that. But Putin believes in God.* Xi Jinping does not believe in God at all. Please listen to this fact carefully.

Jesus Christ is crying about the suppression in China. There are formal Christian churches in China, but they are under the control of the Chinese government. In addition to that, there are underground churches in China. One hundred million people belong to those underground churches. They are in danger now. There are a lot of secret police like there were in East Germany, so Christian people are losing their faith now. In addition to that, I said about Uyghur. It's East Turkistan Republic, they say, but one million to two million people are in re-education camps now. A lot of people are killed under the name of surgery, I mean, their hearts or their kidneys are taken in the name of medical surgery. It's almost like Auschwitz, I think.

Please think about that and trade a lot with China. It's OK that they have an expansionist ambition, but at that time please say to them, "Believe in God. Have faith in God. Give people freedom. Give people democracy. Give people religion. These are the fundamental rights of human beings."

---

* See Chapter 5.

6

Let God Follow Up
On the Lost Jewish People

It's one illustration, one example, but around the world there are other countries like China. We must refuse countries which don't permit the people to believe in God and live like humans. We need freedom. We need democracy. We need religion. So, our movement includes that kind of direction. We will never make a mistake again. In Japan also, I declare that. In Japan, orthodoxly and superficially, people don't want to speak about religion, but in reality, we Happy Science is a subculture of Japan. We are showing direction, for example, guiding the Abe regime to control their direction correctly.

So, please hear my words. The Abe administration is at a loss regarding the relationship between Russia and Japan. It's because of the Ukrainian problem. The EU, especially Germany, dislikes Putin's Russia and its effects reach Japan. Mr. Abe does not have enough relation now, so we Happy Science made a relationship with Donald Trump and Mr. Putin, and we were in contact with Angela Merkel recently.[†] So, we must change the future. We must stop the Third World War.

[†] The author recorded a spiritual interview with the guardian spirit of Chancellor Merkel on September 28, 2018, nine days before this lecture. An excerpt of the recording is included as Chapter 6 in this book.

You regret a lot about the Jewish.
I know you did a lot.
Enough. It's enough!
It's a voice of God. Enough.
Next, it's in charge of God.
Please let God follow up
On the lost Jewish people.
We can, of course.
And please choose to build
A shining, brighter future.
Never make mistake in choice.

7

Stop the Third World War and Believe in the God in Heaven

I said too much. This is the first lecture in Germany, and it includes the U.K. people and the French people here. So, it's a little difficult for me to say the truth, but we must stop the Third World War. It will start from the South China Sea through Xi Jinping's expansionism, his hegemony. It's a problem. So, being kind to them in trading and earning money, it's OK, but say something to them.

"Be democratic.
Give the people liberty, freedom.
And don't kill the people
Who have faith in God."
Even if their name is Islam,
Christianity, Japanese Shintoism,
Or other religions,
In conclusion, they are the same.
There is one Teacher in heaven.
There is one God in heaven.
There is one Father in heaven.
I have been teaching you about that.
Our movement in Europe is still small,
But in this century,
We will change the direction of the world.
Stop the world war
And let the people believe in God.
And live as God loves them.
I ask you like that.

This is my lecture. *Vielen Dank* ("Thank you very much" in German).

Regarding Happy Science Missionary Work in France

Q1

What should be our attitude regarding missionary work in France? Could our faith lessen natural catastrophes in the future?

RYUHO OKAWA

To tell the truth, the Japanese people like the French people more than they do the German people. Before the Second World War, the Japanese people respected the German people a lot, but after that, the Japanese people came to like the French people and admire the French people in the area of, for example, the arts, culture, or fashion. We have a lot of respect for you. And of course, the food.

But we ask you this. The people in France have been lacking philosophy after the Second World War. Their philosophy is like, how do I say, a mathematics-changed philosophy, I mean, they don't think seriously about the rule of human beings or the superior thinking of human beings, but live as it is. This is the tendency of yours. So, the French literature doesn't have enough effects on us now. It's lack of real faith, I think. In another way of saying, it's a decline of the Roman Catholic, I think. The people of France formally believe in Roman Catholicism, but actually, they don't believe in Catholicism. It's from the lack of real spiritualism, I think. They don't know—"they" means the Italian religions and of course the French religions—they lack spiritual thinking. Only exorcism indicates spiritualism, but it's a very small world.

I know a lot about the spiritual world, so it's our turn to teach you about the spiritual world. We know a lot about the spiritual world. Even the Roman Catholics don't know about the real spiritual world and God's Truth. They don't have enough knowledge about, for example, reincarnation or the beginning of life. For example, people believe in the soul, that there is a soul, and its beginning is marriage, they think. But, before that, there are a lot of souls in the heavenly world, so they are waiting to be reborn again into this world. So, the marriage must be sacred regarding this matter. Don't think about this world only. They don't know about the past life and they don't know about the afterlife. Only-this-world thinking and seeking for better life in this world only. It's a tendency of the French and of course other countries of the Western societies. So, "Be spiritual" is important, I think.

The Connection between Beauty, Faith, and Wealth

Q2

In the Q&A session you held in England in 2007, you taught, "Beauty is the gate to the Truth." Please teach us about the connection between beauty, faith, and wealth, so that we can spread the teachings and be happier.

RYUHO OKAWA

Original Christianity is apt to deny earning money and being wealthy. "Being wealthy means you cannot go to heaven. It's very difficult," Jesus said. But it's not enough. His explanation is not enough, I think. Beauty requires a lot of money, of course. If it is a culture-like size, a large size, it requires, of course, some kind of wealthy people's help or something like that. So, in that meaning, if the final destination or the final aim is correct and makes the people happier, money is not bad. It's the same as what Martin Luther in Germany said. For example [*points to his watch on his left wrist*], I have a Lange & Sohne, you know, here in Deutschland. Lange & Sohne was born in Germany, so I wore this today, but this small Lange & Sohne, if I didn't buy this Lange & Sohne, I could have bought a Mercedes-Benz. So, it's your option; which do you like, a Mercedes-Benz or a Lange & Sohne? I preferred a Lange & Sohne because this is Germany and German people will find, "That is a Lange & Sohne! He bought our watch! It's very fantastic." They will think so. So, I did. I would never wear a Lange & Sohne in the U.K. [*laughs*] [*audience laughs*], of course. This is *omotenashi* ("hospitality" in Japanese) of Japan, the Japanese thinking.

So, my answer is "Live diligently. And if you have accumulation of wealth, if you succeed in accumulation of wealth, it means you have the glory of God. At that time, you can change the glory into beauty, and the beauty will lead to the next happiness for other people." OK?

Here, in Deutschland, I held this lecture, but we needed money for it. The Japanese people raised funds, 70 million yen (approx. 650,000 USD), to open this lecture. Thanks to them, it was possible to open this lecture in The Ritz-Carlton hotel, right? If not, I must've had to make a lecture tens or hundreds of times in our branch temple. So, if you live seriously, honestly, and earnestly, succeed in business, earn money, use it for a good direction and make next happiness for people in the name of beauty, it's a great thing, I think. Truth, goodness, and beauty. These three are making new profit in the real meaning in this world, I think. So, don't hesitate to produce beauty. If you walk the right way, it's a great one.

How Can Africa Break Free from Its Status Quo and See the Truth?

Q3

Africa has a history of being colonized, and now, China has an agenda to occupy Africa. What can we do to emancipate Africa from these things, overcome the existing religions, and see the Truth of Happy Science?

RYUHO OKAWA

Ah, OK, OK. [*Audience applauds.*] This is not a lecture in Africa, but I'll answer you.

Firstly, I must say that the first human beings were and are the black people in Africa. This is the starting point of human beings. You can believe and be proud of that. This is the first. The second are the yellow people and the third are the white people. This is the order in which they came to live in this world. So, be proud of that. In the near future, you'll easily understand from The Laws of the Universe. You will really understand about that. It's the first point. (Note: There are people who say that black people were the first immigrants from outer space. According to the spiritual readings by Happy Science, the first humans created on Earth were semi-transparent; they became black in Africa and yellow in Asia. The first earthlings did not take on a definite color, but their color changed depending on where they lived. It should be noted that Queen Sheba of Ethiopia of the Old Testament and Cleopatra of Egypt, both before Jesus' time, were black people. During their time, the white people were considered an inferior race and were sometimes sold as slaves from Europe. Racial problems alternate from one civilization to another. In ancient humankind, there were people with blue skin. Among them were the Dogons, the descendants of people who came from planet Dogon, whose skin were also blue. The blue people were superior when the Dogons were superior.)

The second point is, as you said, colonization by the European people. It was a problem. About 500 years ago, Spanish priests or fathers, or Portuguese fathers, traveled around Africa and examined the people who lived on the African continent and reported to the Vatican that, "The people who live on the African continent are not humans. Don't they have souls?" They reported like that. This was the origin of hatred or discrimination. It's continued till the Second World War. After that, the United States of America won that World War, so they were admired as the champion of democracy and the champion of equality of rights. But in reality, the problem of black people occurred in the 1960s, the President Johnson era. They, the black people, fought against the North Vietnamese people, including the Chinese army, but they didn't have enough civil rights. It was a problem. The origin of democracy, it came from Athens of Greece. Athens had to fight against Persia, which was at that time a gigantic empire. At that time, people who joined in the army of Greece could receive the rights of citizens of Athens. That was the starting point. So, during the Vietnam War, there occurred the black power movement and it changed the world after that. The Japanese army made a failure in the Second World War. In some meaning, they did too much, I think, but in another meaning, after the Second World War, the Pacific War, all the colonies around the Pacific made independence. So partly, we did good and partly, we did bad. It's the conclusion. So, after the economic growth of Japan we must have mercy on all over the world, and must be the champion of solving racism.

But people have reincarnations. I already said that some people are born white, black, or yellow. In the ancient age, the ancient age of

America about 2,000 years ago, there were red people there. But they were perished by another type of white people at that time. There was a great war, but it is not written in history. So, we experienced a lot in several situations. (Note: According to the spiritual readings by Happy Science, the red people who lived on the North American continent were immigrants from Atlantis. They lost to the ancient white people in a nuclear war. Then, those white people lost to the Native Americans.)

Every person has a reason for returning back to this world, but no person can understand the real meaning till they say goodbye to this world. So, while you are living in this world, please think, think, and think, thinking on and on and on and on. "What is the reason of my living and the reality?" Also, please think and believe in the law of cause and effect. If you did good things, your future will be better. If not in this world, in the next world, you will get the fruits of good things. But even if you are rich and celebrated by other people, and superficially live happily in this world, if in reality, you have seeds of evil and people receive the seeds of evil from you, your next life will be a very sad one, I think. So, even if all of you cannot explain what you are, who you are, your economic stage, family problem, or another thing, the past cannot be changed, but you can change your mind and start the law of cause and effect, and you'll be better and better in the near future. I can promise about this thing. It's a reality, of course. So, be hopeful about that.

Vielen Dank. Auf Wiedersehen ("Thank you very much. See you again" in German).

The Fact and the Truth

Lecture given on May 22, 2011
at Kowloonbay International Trade & Exhibition Centre
Hong Kong

1

Liberty is a Chance of Prosperity

Good evening, Hong Kong. Just last night, I came back from the Philippines. In the Philippines, I spoke in a large voice, so my throat is destroyed today. I'm very sorry for all of you. [*Audience applauds.*] Thank you, thank you very much. Today, I will speak in a low voice and in a slow voice. But this is just the first time for me, so you are very lucky to hear me in such kind of voice. Almost all of the people in the world can never hear my lecture with a voice like this, so you are very lucky today.

Late last night, I went back to my hotel in Hong Kong and astonishingly, I found that my movie, *The Laws of Eternity**, was on TV, on-air, just at that time. I thank you for your cooperation and your efforts. You did a lot for me. I'm very thankful to you about that. This is a very beautiful movie and I love it very much indeed.

Before leaving Japan for Hong Kong, I studied about Hong Kong through a movie. Its name is *Body Guards and Assassins*†, you know, about Sun Wen? *Sombun no Gishidan* in Japanese. I hope you are not assassins. You are bodyguards for me, I hope so. I came here just to declare that the prosperity of Hong Kong is very much

---

* An animated movie produced and directed by Ryuho Okawa, released in 2006.

† Beijing Poly-bona Film Publishing Company and Cinema Popular, 2009.

important in the prosperity of the future of China. You have been changing in these 14 years since you were returned from Great Britain to China. The Japanese have been looking at you, how Hong Kong has changed in recent years. At this time, you are running at top speed in Asia, as the first runner of the prosperity of Asia. It's a very happy thing for me.

Today, I dare ask you. You have now a very precious thing, a very precious value in you. Its name is liberty. Liberty and equality are sometimes thought as two conflicting values. But it's a little different, I think. Liberty is the equality of prosperity for everybody. It's a chance of prosperity. It's a chance to participate in something. It's a chance to get money and make a successful life in you. I think if you must choose one value between liberty and equality, you must choose liberty first. In liberty, there is equality of choice. Equality of choice to prosper, equality of choice to make efforts, and every chance is there in front of you, in the future of your country, I think. So, between these two values, there is no conflict indeed. Firstly, you should choose liberty. In addition, I add that we and you human beings are happy because you have your freedom of thinking in you. It's not enabled for anyone to deprive you of it. Freedom of thinking, freedom of speech, freedom of publication, and freedom to believe in something valuable are very essential for human beings.

2

Lessons to Be Learned from Japan

Last night I thought that in Hong Kong, you can watch *The Laws of Eternity* on TV, but in Japan, only *The Golden Laws** can be seen at the present because the Japanese people suffered from a 9.0-magnitude earthquake, a tsunami, and the aftermath of that—the syndrome of nuclear reactors problem. I have other famous movies, *The Laws of the Sun* and *The Rebirth of Buddha*, and they were scheduled to be on air in Japan this April and May, but in those movies, there was a scene of a tsunami, so in Japan we could not air those kinds of films. But in Hong Kong, you could see *The Laws of Eternity*. In that TV, I was astonished that you could produce a commercial of the event today. My face was on TV. Oh, it's astonishing to me. In Japan, it's very difficult because if TV aired my face, my name, and my books or my lectures like in Hong Kong, people would receive too much influence from that TV commercial. It's very difficult, even in Japan.

So, nowadays Japan is a socialist country [*laughs*] and you, Hong Kong is the country of liberty. It's quite different. In Japan people are fearful of the differences between people—the differences between the poor and the rich, and the differences between the people who

---

* *The Golden Laws* (2003), *The Laws of the Sun* (2000), and *The Rebirth of Buddha* (2009) are all animated movies produced and directed by Ryuho Okawa.

succeeded in their lives and the people who failed in their lives. There are almost no such kind of poor-level people in Japan of course, but on the contrary to that, there are not so much rich people in Japan. You are very rich in Hong Kong. I admire the fact. You are very rich people in spite of the main policy of your mother country, China. People of Hong Kong are rich and have a lot of good entertainment. In Japan, people think that they are protecting capitalism and freedom of the market, but it's not true.

In the recent 20 years, Japan made a lot of mistakes. One is that they made great pressure on the Japanese economy. They said that, they mean the Japanese mass media and its supporters, they supported the pressure on the bubble economy of Japan to perish it. After that, the Japanese people suffered from depression of economy or declining of the economy in these 20 years. In that time, great China was becoming greater and greater in economy and last year, China replaced Japan on the GDP basis. You became No. 2, second place in the world. It's a blessing. I bless you so much. You made great efforts in your growth of economy. And in these 20 years, Japan made another mistake. It is said *yutori kyoiku* in Japanese, it means "to loosen" the education. It means to lessen the competition in education. So, the textbooks of children in elementary school, junior high school, and senior high school became thinner and thinner. In junior high school, the compulsory education used to require (students to learn) more than 500 English words, but in these two decades in Japan, only 100 English words were required. It led the competition ability of Japan in the direction of decline.

These two mistakes led to the depression of economy, the status quo of depression of Japan now. So, I tell you, "Never give up. Study harder and harder." I've heard that the Chinese people, of course including the people in Hong Kong, are good at studying English very much. It's very clever of you. If you want to become richer and richer and if you want to make a successful life, you must learn harder and harder. The pavement to hell is made from goodwill. Small children and younger people hesitate to study harder and harder, but it leads your country to decline. So, be patient to study. Continue studying English and other language, and other subjects. It's a lesson from Japan.

3
Peace is Required for Great Economic Growth

And you Chinese people, including Hong Kong and Shanghai, will confront the difficulties in economy in the near future. It will be called as bubble economy like it was in Japan, and sometimes the authority and mass media will speak loud, how it's important to give pressure to the bubble economy and to make a normal economy. They will be inclined to say so. But it's the same way that the Japanese people walked. So, at that time, be patient and stop and think. Make up your mind, change your mind to direct your country upward. You can be greater and greater. You can be twice, three times, or more as great as you are. You are a promised country. Your authorities are thinking in their mind that, in the year 2016, your gross national product must catch up to the United States of America. In some meaning, it's possible. But it requires additional conditions. One condition is, economy, especially world economy, requires peace in the world. Being peaceful is required to make great growth in economy. So, to be peaceful is first, and the second is the growth of the economy. If there will occur some kind of conflicts between large countries, world economies are going to decline and will not be able to widen its size.

We are now thinking how to remake the Japanese economy and the Japanese political authority again. This 11th the March, the great earthquake and the tsunami destroyed the east part of Japan. But it is not the end for Japan because there is Happy Science, the headquarters of Happy Science. Happy Science includes the science of happiness. It means how to make happiness in every field. So, we are supporting in the political meaning, in the educational meaning, and in the economic meaning. We will stand up again in these 3 years and make good competition with other great countries which have leaderships now.

I now dare add to that. You, China, have become one of the great leaders of the world. Be sure about that. We, the Japanese don't have envy about that. We congratulate you on that. We, the Japanese people want to become good friends with you and have co-relationship, co-existence, and co-growth in economy and in politics. We, Japan and the United States of America are friends in the political meaning, diplomatic meaning, and economic meaning, but I think we, China and Japan must be friends from now on and continue to be so. If we become enemies like such kind in *Body Guards and Assassins*, it's a loss for the world, not only economic, but also a political loss.

4

Be Humble in front of Heavenly Beings

So, I just ask you. You already saw in the movie *The Laws of Eternity* that there are different dimensional worlds. They are beyond this three-dimensional world. These have been taught in Buddhism and the Japanese people were taught Buddhism from ancient China. In return, we Happy Science, as a new Buddhism, shall teach you about that. Other dimensions, the fourth dimension, the fifth dimension and beyond that which are pictured in the movie, are real. They are real, it's the Truth.

We, Happy Science, are science, and in front of science, there spread the unknown worlds. One of the unknown worlds is the spiritual world. The spiritual world is in itself an existence. So, from now on we are seeking for the real fact in this world and in another situation, or from another point of view, we are seeking for other dimensional world, the spiritual world which was taught by the ancient Chinese people. So, these two eyes are required now.

Only human beings can believe in the beings beyond humans. They are called God, Buddha, or angels. Animals cannot think about them. So, it's a scientific attitude. Don't think it's a superstition. Don't think that it's just a fiction. It is a reality. I published almost 700 books (at the time of the lecture), and in these books I wrote a lot about another world. It has been written about in these 25 years. I'm now concerned whether this truth can be understood in Hong Kong and spread from Hong Kong to all over China. I hope it can. This is a condition of a human being. Being humble in front of heavenly beings will promise you to become greater and greater in the near future. I hope so. I came here as a messenger of peace. Thank you very much.

About the Mayan Prediction of the End of the World

Q1

Many people are asking me and asking the world what's happening. Yesterday, many people spoke about the apocalypse happening. Our Mayan friends are talking about 2012. The world is changing, and many people are afraid and confused. I want to understand your view on what might be happening. Orbs of light showing up when they take photos, these kinds of things.

RYUHO OKAWA

OK. OK. There was a movie, *2012*[*]. It pictured about the the day of the end of the world. There might be produced a lot of other movies regarding 2012. After the Nostradamus prediction of 1999, the Mayan prediction of the end of the world is 2012. It must become some kind of move in pictures, science fiction, and some kind of novels. But I dare say nothing shall happen because there's Happy Science. I now came down here to stop the worrying of the world, to stop the destroying of the world, to stop the bad predictions of the world. This world, this age will not pass without us spreading our teachings of Happy Science. You can be sure about that.

I came here to tell the Truth. There shall be no ending, no end of the world because I have my mission. My mission has not ended. My mission has just started. I lost my clear voice today. It's a disaster for you, the people of Hong Kong, but my will to save the world will not be perished on earth from now on. I promise we can conquer any crisis. Some kind of crises will occur in some size or grade, but we can conquer such kind of difficulties because we have a lot of powers. There are a lot of people in the world. We can cooperate. We can cooperate and our cooperating power will produce the almighty power of God. It's OK. No problem.

---

[*] Columbia Pictures, 2009.

How Can I Share My Mission and Love to Everybody?

Q2

I have been reading your books for 10 years and now I finally got to meet you. I would like to ask you, how can I be like you? You're full of light, you're so charming. Also, how can I share my belief in El Cantare*, my mission to spread it, and the love to everybody I know? Please teach me and teach everyone.

RYUHO OKAWA

OK. Thank you very much. Hong Kong is famous for its food. Its food is No. 1 as Chinese food, I've heard, and I tasted, I examined, and I was proven like that. It's true. I came here to Hong Kong, this is the third time for me to come here, Hong Kong. Firstly, I came in 1996, next, in recent times when I came back from India this March, and this is the third time for me to come here. I love the people of Hong Kong and I love the Chinese people because you have one-fifth of the population of the world. It's a great, great country and it will determine the direction of the world destiny, I mean. So, no one can deny you.

Especially, I rely on the people of Hong Kong. You were promised to continue the constitution, the status quo from the Great Britain age to maybe around the year 2050 or so. But almost all of the people of the world are thinking that you will be absorbed in the great China, and that you, the people of Hong Kong will also become a different type of people who don't like success and who are inclined to engaged in agriculture, fishing, or things like that. However, I don't think so. People who have experienced prosperity never forget about that. People who have experienced a lot about prosperity will teach other people how to prosper in this world. You

---

*El Cantare is the highest grand spirit of the terrestrial spirit group, and is a spirit from the ninth dimension which has been guiding humanity from the creation of Earth. He is the Supreme God of the Earth that Jesus called Father and Muhammad called Allah. A part of its core consciousness has descended to Earth as Ryuho Okawa. See the section, "What is El Cantare?" in the end pages of this book.

are the teachers. You are one portion of great China, but you are the teachers of great China, and you can teach all Chinese people. And you are the leaders of the Chinese people.

So, if I can put some kind of mission and some kind of responsibility on you, and you accept that responsibility to enlighten all the people in China and can show the direction of the future of China, it would be welcomed by people all over the world. I think the Chinese people themselves should determine their destiny, so you have the right to determine your destiny. But you need some teacher about that. Its teacher is, I think, the people of Hong Kong. You can teach the more-than-one-billion population of China. They will follow you. So, you yourself, the people of Hong Kong, change and other Chinese will change after that.

The most anxious thing for me is the confrontation. It's the conflict between China and the United States of America including Japan. We must change such kind of future. We must be friends. So, it depends on our will. If the people of Hong Kong can lead a lot of Chinese people to the future, you can remake this country and make happier and happier the people of this country. They need some kind of teachers, I think, and you can be the teachers. And we just can assist you in the meaning of the spiritual point and in the meaning of "how to think in the scientific meaning." So, it depends on China, China's prosperity, and peaceful China. The world's peace and the world's prosperity depend on if peaceful China can be realized in the future or not. We must be friends with all the people of the world, so we must forgive each other, we must nurture each other, and we must instruct each other. I hope so. And I think we can. Yes, we can.

Where in the Spirit World Are Political Figures from China and Taiwan?

Q3

I just want to know, the spirits of Sun Wen, Chiang Kai-shek, Koxinga* and other political figures from China and from Taiwan, are they also here tonight? Where are those political figures? Are they now in heaven or somewhere else, and what are they doing now? Are they now trying to guide someone to do some work or some political parties? What are they actually doing now for the cross-Strait relationship between Taiwan and China? So, please can you give me some comments?

RYUHO OKAWA

It's regarding the history of China, Hong Kong and Taiwan. Sun Wen, he was a great man. Now, he is in the heavenly world, and one of the Nyorai (Tathagata). I say, in our words, he is in the eighth dimensional world. He came here, maybe in 1906, in preparation for a revolution, but he took a lot of risks and fought against the old regime. He is now in a high position in the great hierarchy of politicians in the Spirit World, and he is giving light to this world. He is thinking about, of course, Taiwan, Hong Kong, Shanghai, and around Beijing and other areas of China. This is a great country, so it's very difficult to make one direction.

There are of course other politicians who have great missions. I don't know the exact names, how to say in English, but you have a lot of great leaders like the Meiji Restoration of Japan had. You have a lot of great political people in this country. They are thinking together, and will lead your country to the happier side. I can rely on them. You became such kind of great-population country in these days. It means in this third dimensional world, you have been successful. And when people get success in this world, people seek for another

---

*Sun Wen (Sun Yat-sen) (1866–1925) was a Chinese revolutionary and thinker who became the first provisional president of the Republic of China when the Xinhai Revolution occurred in 1911. Chiang Kai-shek (1887–1975) was the first president of the Republic of China. Defeated by the Communist Party of China led by Mao Zedong after WWII, he fled to Taiwan in 1949. Koxinga (1624–1662) was a military personnel and a politician of the Ming dynasty. He is sometimes considered "one of the three national gods" in Taiwan, along with Sun Wen and Chiang Kai-shek, after having defeated the Dutch forces in Formosa (currently Taiwan).

value. It's a mental value, or it exceeds the mental value—the divine value or eternal value, I think.

When I came here, I also read about the author of *The Importance of Living*, Lin Yutang*. He was born in the south part of China. He went abroad to the United States of America and studied at Harvard University, went back to China, became the professor of Peking University, and died here in Hong Kong. His book about the importance of living was read all over the world and he received a lot of respect from the people of the world because he was not only intelligent, but also had a lot of humor in his essays and in his writings. So, I hope there will be more and more humor in the Chinese people. It's a strong point of the Chinese people. In terms of humor, you are superior to the Japanese people, you are superior to the German people, and you are superior to people of other countries. So, economic growth and humor will make you happier and happier. In this place Hong Kong, I will add another teaching. In human life, we need humor, and it will make people reconcile and rebuild their lives in the future.

I cannot answer all of your questions correctly, but I'm sure that you have a lot of angels of light in heaven regarding politics, and they are thinking and leading you now, so I can rely on them. In addition to that, your strongest point is humor. Please add humor as you spread your country's strategy. Please spread Chinese humor all

---

* Lin Yutang (1895–1976) was a renowned Chinese writer, translator, linguist, philosopher, and inventor.

over the world. I hope so. It's happier and happier for other people in the world. I think Chinese humor is required now. You are too much serious about everything, like the Japanese.

Chapter THREE

Love Beyond Hatred

Lecture given on March 3, 2019
at Grand Hyatt Taipei
Taipei, Taiwan

1
Happy Science Is Changing the World through Its Opinion

I was last here in Taiwan eleven years ago[*] and am truly delighted to be here again. This trip had not been in my plans, at first. But in early February (2019), I received a set of autobiographical DVDs and a letter by your former president, Mr. Lee Teng-hui[†]. I have already written him a letter of gratitude in response, but while I was reading his letter, I saw that his words were brimming with concern for the future of Taiwan. Even at his unyoung age of 96, he humbly expressed to me the hope he lays upon me, a much younger person, to help his country.

I don't know how much there is I can do to help but I thought that, perhaps, I can help to bridge Japan and Taiwan, and Taiwan and continental China. Thousands of Happy Science believers are here in Taiwan, and thousands more also live in the People's Republic of China (the PRC), where strained relations have existed with Taiwan. Our heart-to-heart communication between our

---

[*] The author had previously given a lecture titled, "The Realization of Buddhaland Utopia" at Happy Science Taipei Local Temple, in Taiwan, on November 9, 2008. An excerpt of the lecture is included in Further Reading at the end of this chapter.

[†] Lee Teng-hui (1923–present) is a Taiwanese statesman who was born in Taiwan during Japanese rule. He studied at schools such as Kyoto Imperial University, National Taiwan University, and Cornell University. Later, he pursued a career in politics and served as the president of Taiwan from 1988 to 2000.

believers have reached beyond national borders, and I am the Master of this religious organization of followers in both countries.

We hold activities in more than 105 countries around the world, among which there exist friendly relations as well as conflicting interests. But I have continued my work to this very day in hopes that the teachings leading to the faith at Happy Science will bring the people of this world together. It's uncertain how far we'll manage to reach, but I can say that the opinions I give as an individual or publish as an author hold the most influence, at least in Japan, where the lectures I've given around the world are reproduced in many Japanese newspapers. When I went in October of last year to give a lecture in Berlin, Germany,[‡] and I appealed to the audience about the severe situation of the Uyghur region in the PRC where more than one million people are suffering from brainwashing education inside internment camps, several days later, the existence of these internment camps became officially acknowledged by the Beijing administration. News of this then became published in newspapers around the world, including in Japan.

I believe in the importance of discussing topics that should be discussed when they come to our minds because I've seen things like this occur. I'm certain you have probably noticed that, we, Happy Science, seek to teach about what is right beyond religious differences. So if, by any chance, people in other parts of the world

---

[‡] See Chapter 1.

are suffering under unreasonable circumstances, we wish to alleviate their suffering as much as possible; if people of other countries are absorbed by their own hatred, then we also wish to ease their hatred and encourage them to develop their countries based on the heart of love, and we have used the peaceful means of free speech to do so.

When the people of Japan in the post-WWII era long gave up the effort to think, Happy Science emerged out of such times to show Japan which direction it should head toward. The current Japanese administration led by the Liberal Democratic Party of Japan, the majority party, has only been in fact, implementing ideas originally proposed by Happy Science and the Happiness Realization Party, the political party of the Happy Science Group, two to three years earlier.

Today's event may seem very modest, but in due time, more than one hundred countries around the world will be shown the contents of this lecture. This indeed is an incredible thing. Countries all around the world will be shared what I have discussed in this lecture, and so I ask you not to look at this religious power too lightly. We are also persistent. Because of our great persistence, we don't easily give in. We persist, and persist, and continue forth, even when public opinion drifts in the opposite direction, creating strong unfavorable winds. We don't hesitate to speak our mind when we believe something is not right.

My honest sense of things eleven years ago, when I came to Taiwan at the start of President Ma's administration, was that Taiwan was in a crisis. A sense of apprehension for the safety of

Taiwan's future filled me. Taiwan would fall into the hands of Beijing's wishes if things were to continue as they were, and I was extremely worried about this. This was the same time when, in Japan, the Democratic Party of Japan—formerly an opposition party—became the ruling party, and eventually put three prime ministers in office starting in 2009. So when I saw the wrong direction that this leadership was heading our country toward, I created the Happiness Realization Party and voiced my fierce criticism about this administration. In due course, the Democratic Party's administration came to an end in just three years to give way to the current administration led by Prime Minister Abe.

In this way, Happy Science dares to do things that others normally wouldn't. Perhaps we do not have enough capacity yet, but it is my belief that our passion, eagerness, and persistence to continue do not in the least pale in comparison to other organizations. Above all else, we first think about what is righteous from the perspective of God or Buddha. There are law-governed nations in this world, for example, that determine rightness based on their laws, and they enforce their people to abide by them as if doing so is completely natural. The PRC as well as the Republic of China, which is Taiwan, practices this.

Even in such law-governed nations, however, it is important to consider whether the laws were created based on the mind of God or Buddha. A nation's laws need to have been created to lead its people to happiness, not to serve the self-interests of politicians who hold no regard for the mind of God or Buddha. Being a law-governed nation doesn't automatically make the nation alright. What is of true importance is that those who create the country's laws are actually living and working in accordance with the will of God.

2

Which Is the Righteous Side, Taiwan or China?

In my preparation for coming here, I held many spiritual interviews[*] with leaders[†] who have been involved in the China-Taiwan divide after Sun Yat-sen's revolution. This included those whose souls are still living, in which cases, it was their guardian spirits—their soul siblings[‡]—who spoke these messages. Many of these have been published, and some of them, perhaps, have yet to be translated into Chinese, but at least, they most likely have been released as videos.

As a result of them, I came to basically understand that the movement which started with Sun Yat-sen, who is called the father of the country in both Taiwan and the PRC, and other leaders such

---

[*] See the end section of the book.

[†] Okawa had previously recorded spiritual interviews with Sun Yat-sen, Chiang Kai-shek, and the guardian spirits of Lee Teng-hui and Tsai Ing-wen.

[‡] In principle, the human soul consists of six parts or "soul siblings"; one core and five branch souls. When a soul is born into this world as a human being, one of its soul siblings serves as its guardian spirit. See the end section of the book.

as Chiang Kai-shek, Lee Teng-hui, and Tsai Ing-wen** who came after him, is the one that represents the righteous line. This is what I came to truly understand as I saw that many people from this movement have returned to the higher reaches of heaven. This may not be true of all of them. Perhaps some were a little different.

In contrast, there is the PRC, which has grown as a country and gained military power, economic development, and widespread political influence across the globe. But I have regrettably found that the movement created by Mao Zedong, Deng Xiaoping—the leader of the Chinese Economic Reform—and Mr. Xi Jinping of our present times, had ideas differing from the will of God or Buddha which we believe in. This is, in fact, the harsh truth.

In February, I held a lecture on the book, *Spiritual Interview with Mao Zedong* in the Japanese city of Nagoya. Indeed, I held this in Japan, in the city of Nagoya, completely in Japanese, for a Japanese audience. But even then, the spirit of Mao Zedong came to me while I was there, eagerly pressuring me to cancel this lecture, as it was causing him distress.

Then, also, before setting out to come here this morning, I was visited by the guardian spirit of Mr. Xi Jinping who also tried to negotiate with me to cancel this lecture. His visit didn't last very long; perhaps it lasted about thirteen minutes, which we made sure

---

** Tsai Ing-wen (1956–present) is a Taiwanese politician and a member of the Democratic Progressive Party who became the first female president and the 14th-term president of Taiwan in 2016.

to take a recording of. Over the course of his visit, he kept trying to convince us to call off this lecture. In response, we explained that an audience of over 900 people planning to come today would scarcely impact him, in comparison to the 1.4 billion people living in the PRC. Holding this lecture would be similar to throwing a pebble, hardly any cause for his concern. But he denied this, insisting the impact will gradually spread and the information that will reach him from various sources will bother him. He continued trying to negotiate, insisting I avoid topics that would cause him trouble and saying he would be pleased the most to see this lecture called off. That he would be so distressed by a lecture of this scale truly amazed me. I could imagine that holding it at the Tiananmen Square may leave some impact, but I found, to my surprise, that having it in Taiwan for a mainly Taiwanese audience bothered him that much.

Everyone, of course, has the freedom to choose their own thinking and various experiments should be permitted as they practice their ideas in their government, looking for ways to better serve the development and prosperity of their country. However, we are living in modern times. We now live neither in the age of feudalism nor the age of warring states. That having greater might, military power, and strength enables the weaker to be forced into capitulation, or that might is right, are ideas no longer accepted by modern society. We mustn't overlook this fact. The international community may, at times, allow such things to take place, but this will not always be the case, and this deserves careful thought.

3

The Issue with Totalitarian China

Shortly before my coming here, a summit meeting was held in Hanoi, Vietnam, between U.S. President Donald Trump and North Korea's head Mr. Kim Jong-un (February 27 to 28). There's been word that these talks will be continued, but what had virtually happened was the collapse of their diplomatic relationship, which might have been a favorable outcome for Taiwan. President Trump was predicted in prior forecasts to offer considerable concessions to North Korea, and I was concerned for the great danger Taiwan may face if the U.S. President, Donald Trump, goes to great lengths to travel to Vietnam, once an enemy state and the site of the Vietnam War, and chooses to treat Mr. Kim Jong-un as an equal or more than an equal by offering him concessions.

But it seems that Mr. Trump hasn't resorted to doing this and has held his ground. If the U.S. were to ever accept North Korea into discussions on equal footing, or if North Korea were ever permitted an equal level of a war of words, the U.S. will see a significant decline in its influence over future talks between Taiwan and the PRC. The economic power (GDP size) of Mr. Kim Jong-un's country is only 1/1,100 of that of the United States but he does not actually understand this. He believes that even with an economy of this size, building hydrogen and atomic bombs will give him equal power to fight the United States. It can be seen here how he lacks in his thinking as a leader. A democratic nation will see that a leader who allows many of his people to suffer from starvation, limits their political freedom, and sometimes places them in internment camps, all the while obsessively creating hydrogen bombs, should be urged severe repentance. For the U.S. to offer too many reconciliations would be an unfit thing to do. It seems that President Trump is trying to promote Mr. Kim Jong-un's better understanding of things and foster a peaceful resolution.

North Korea needs to know that it is not on equal footing with the United States. When your leadership is heading your country into unfavorable circumstances or a future of sorrow and suffering, a democracy allows the leader to be replaced through the system of election. This allows a permanent revolution, in a sense. People can change their government into a new one without the sacrifice of a single human life and this is exemplar of the concept that gives sovereignty to the people. A country that does not have such a system, and instead, suppresses, purges, or slaughters people who try to bring changes to it, is basically taking away the people's free speech, free press, freedom of politics, and freedom of religious faith. This may seem like one type of value system that can be chosen, but the truth is that it shouldn't be considered an option at all because from the broader perspective of our modern society, we should aim to create political and economic systems that lead to the happiness of as many people as possible.

Some, after World War II, have looked upon this war as a conflict between democracy and fascism*. In a strict sense, however, this wasn't the case. For example, it became very clear after the war that the Soviet Union had also been a fascist country like Germany and Italy during World War II. I would like to explain how to make this distinction. A totalitarian country says that the citizens exist for the sake of the country and considers their people to be their servants. And when one has not shown their service to one's country, it can be decided whether this person is to live or perish. For a country of a united cause to survive, it is allowed to limit the rights of the people and suppress them. These are the characteristics that define a totalitarian country.

Also, the American political philosopher, Hannah Arendt, pointed out three signs of a totalitarian country. The first sign is a secret or special police force keeping the country's citizens under surveillance. The second sign is the existence of internment camps where people who resist against or politically criticize the administration are imprisoned and forced into silence. Camps like these are used to isolate people from the public. The third sign is a system of purging or the slaughtering of people. People who are seen as nuisances to the administration's interests are mercilessly

---

*Fascism is the term for a political regime with totalitarian tendencies that appeared after World War I. In many cases, it's a single-party dictatorship with belligerent policies. Fascism originated with the Revolutionary Fascist Party of Italy, then later spread to Germany and Spain.

purged and erased from this world without due trial in court. When a country is seen to have all three of these things—a secret police, internment camps, and a system of purging—this signifies a totalitarian country. None of these signs have been found so far, in Taiwan, and your country, in this sense, is not a totalitarian state, but a country founded on the western principles of freedom, democracy, and faith.

At first glance, the PRC, your neighboring country, with its large population and developed economy, may seem like an ideal place. But since the time Hong Kong was reverted to the PRC, the Hong Kong people have faced difficult lives, suppressed freedom, and an uncertain future. This is not something that should surprise us. While Hong Kong's handover brought more than 150 years of British sovereignty (1842 to 1997) to a close, their people have since faced impoverishment and the suppression of freedom, and these conditions have led to the Umbrella Revolution, showing that a reversion shouldn't automatically signify that the ruling country is allowed to have its way with the acquired region.

What is more, a leading country of the world like the PRC should have more understanding about the rest of the world and a better awareness of how it's being perceived by the international community. The problem in the PRC boils down to a single point, which is Mr. Xi Jinping's lack of global awareness. His country should have seen more changes than it has thus far if he had been better at reading and understanding the international society and situation. The many spiritual interviews with his guardian spirit[*] which I have held, published, and discussed my opinions about, came from my wish to foster this change.

The terrible state that the country of North Korea faces now, is the result of modeling their country after the PRC. They followed the PRC's military-first policy and failed to transition their country into a market economy. The economic growth that the PRC possesses now came as a result of Deng Xiaoping's pleas to the business leaders in Japan to come to the PRC, build factories of higher production capabilities, and teach his people how to create more wealth. When the Great Leap Forward policy and the Cultural Revolution failed, and then came the death of Mao Zedong, Deng Xiaoping went to these business leaders in Japan, humbly seeking for their help. Responding with their earnest support, they relocated their production bases and set up factories in the PRC.

The growth of the Chinese people's GDP was an outcome of these Japanese business leaders' efforts to strengthen the Chinese economy. But on the political spectrum, the PRC continued to follow the Marxism-Leninism system, even if just formally. The Japanese model was followed in some ways but not in others, in this way. So, even after economic growth was achieved, the military-first policy sown by Mao Zedong was continued and has now become the source of a global-scale problem.

---

[*] See Ryuho Okawa, *China's Hidden Agenda: The Mastermind behind the Anti-American and Anti-Japanese Protests* (Tokyo: HS Press, 2012) and Chapter 4 of this book.

4

Spread the Freedom, Democracy, and Faith of Taiwan to Mainland China

On yesterday's front page of a Japanese newspaper called the *Sankei Shimbun*, an article[*] was printed about an interview at the government-general of Taiwan, held between President Tsai Ing-wen and the paper's managing editor from the Tokyo head office. A part of this article was also published in this morning's local English-language and Chinese-language newspapers.

The same issue will follow regardless of whom you choose as your leader. This issue is not a matter of just choosing between the Democratic Progressive Party and the Nationalist Party. As I explained earlier, a totalitarian nation is clearly different from a democratic country. In a totalitarian country, the people are sacrificed for the sake of their country. In a democratic country, on the other hand, it is the duty of the country to realize the happiness of its people. The country's leaders and government officials should be civil servants whose job is to realize the happiness of their people. Should they ever fail to do so, their people are allowed to remove

---

[*] *Sankei Shimbun* printed an article on its exclusive interview with President Tsai Ing-wen in its March 2, 2019 edition. In the interview, President Tsai expressed, for the first time, her hope to have talks with the Japanese government over security issues prompted by the increasing PRC threat.

them from their posts, regardless of whether they are a politician, a government official in high office, or of any other government level. This is the shape of democracy.

In this sense, Taiwan's culture is clearly different from that of the PRC. A different civilization exists here, in Taiwan. Ms. Tsai Ing-wen is cautiously avoiding the use of the word "independence" in order to avoid Beijing's hard-lining diplomacy and unfavorable treatment against Taiwan. Her words have been chosen carefully and to speak abstractly, for this reason.

But there is no need to fight for your independence. Your country has continued to grow as its own independent nation and is a country of its own. I ask of Taiwan to spread throughout the PRC your ideas of prosperity and development, the principles of democracy, freedom, and capitalist ideas, and your spirit of cherishing religious faith, for doing so will bring happiness to many people there. The people of Hong Kong are suffering terribly right now, and I would like to find some way to help them. Perhaps there is little room to think of anything other than your own country right now. But if the people of Hong Kong are on the verge of facing terrible circumstances in the future, I hope you will find it in yourself the wish to help them.

These are the things I hope we'll be able to accomplish. Please choose political systems that will bring people happiness, not suffering. I clearly want to say that the people of a nation hold the responsibility, duty, and the right to create and construct such systems.

5

Uniting the U.S., Japan, and Taiwan to Protect the Freedom of the Indo-Pacific Region

As I say this, I admit that the Japanese have not been clearly expressing their opinions and discussing them as much as they should. In 1972, former Japanese Prime Minister Kakuei Tanaka revived diplomatic relations with the PRC and unilaterally severed relations with Taiwan. I feel that this was a very embarrassing event that, at least, was a decision that a nation of the bushido spirit should not have made. There isn't a problem with the Japanese developing diplomatic relations with the PRC, now that it has grown into a large country. There isn't anything wrong with the PRC seeking diplomatic ties with the Japanese, either. But the PRC's territorial claim on Taiwan is just the opinion of the PRC, not that of the Japanese.

So building Japanese ties with the PRC should not have led to unilaterally abandoning their ties with Taiwan. Many Taiwanese soldiers fought as Japanese nationals in World War II and perished, and their souls have been commemorated in the Yasukuni Shrine in Japan. Considering this, I feel Japan's decision to end relations with Taiwan out of sensitivity to China to have been embarrassing.

Japan should have made a decision based on what they believed to be righteous from their own standpoint, but they couldn't, which has now led to the very unstable future that Taiwan faces. Our power may not be enough, but we, Happy Science, or the Happiness Realization Party, have worked actively to foster what I've been talking about. The Happiness Realization Party is in strong support of restoring diplomatic relations between Japan and Taiwan, and insists further on the need to build an alliance. We believe that combining strength and forming a trilateral alliance between Japan, Taiwan, and the United States to protect the free world of the Indo-Pacific will also bring a positive impact to the rest of the world.

It's my hope that the values we support are also spread to continental China. The people of continental China are facing constant video surveillance and mobile- and smart-phone monitoring by the government. This is a country exactly like the future society depicted in George Orwell's novel, *1984*, but there are people who haven't realized about this. I believe God and those who believe in Him should tell them that this is not how a country should be.

Please do not fear, though. The people of Japan will not let you down this time. The country of Japan is now on the verge of change. Japan will shortly have a joint defense system with the United States to prepare not only for invasions on Japan itself, but also for possible foreign invasions into the Taiwan Strait, the South China Sea, the East China Sea, and namely, toward Filipino and Vietnamese territory. This transition should happen fairly soon. It's true that North Korea has been developing nuclear weapons capability. But Japan has been capable of doing this at any time should it have chosen to do so; it just hasn't chosen to yet.

Japan has enough technology to easily develop nuclear weapons capability in just two years. It just hasn't done so, so as to avoid rifts in diplomatic relations and for maintaining peace throughout Asia as much as possible. Should someone like Mr. Kim Jong-un ignore the United States' requests and choose to do as he wishes, Japan may need to reconsider this stance.

At the least, it's my belief that Japan should hold a certain degree of responsibility in Taiwan's future. Reading Mr. Lee Teng-hui's letter and seeing this 96-year-old gentleman's concern about the future made me realize that I needed to tell you what Japan will do. This is how I came to discuss my thoughts about this subject today.

6
My Words Are Not a Prophecy, but God's Plans

I have talked about things that have not been realized into the present, but they will come to fruition in the next two or three years' time, or at least within ten years from now. For the future society will be built upon my words.

The future will be opened in the direction my words point to. This is the reality that has manifested thus far and shall be the reality that will manifest from here on. Perhaps many people are hoping to hear me prophesy the future. But I have talked about not a prophecy, but God's plans, God's thoughts, God's very wishes. The world shall head in this direction.

From here on, we, Japanese, will not forsake Taiwan, and we are willing to fulfill our duty. Japan is building its strength to fulfill this end. Please have the courage to voice and insist on what you believe to be righteous and think to yourselves that your future will be created by your own hands. It's not good for an age to last a long time where people have to tip-toe around the feelings and sentiments of foreign countries and let these things determine how they choose their words. Those belonging to free countries ought to say the things that ought to be said out loud.

7

Cast Aside All Hatred and Embrace Love

Please understand that God's and Buddha's teachings are above the laws and constitutions of human beings. Japan changed its constitution after World War II, but something was forgotten in the process. In America and in European countries, people wrote the laws of the land, created a parliament, made decisions, and conducted government based on Christian values. That is to say, their democracy was based on religious faith.

The politicians of Japan have failed to remember this and so have many members of the mass media. My wish, at this present, is to restore us to the original style. I hereon firmly deny a future in which the lives of the people of Taiwan are faced with suffering. If you encounter hardships that you don't know what to do about, please come to us, Happy Science. We will do everything that we can do to help.

In Japan, we have the most influential of opinions and are the most willing to speak our opinions to the world. Earlier, I raised the region of Uyghur as an example. They are facing miserable conditions. Even though they are considered an autonomous region, 1.2 million people are imprisoned inside internment camps and another 2 million go there to receive reeducation, a brainwashing education. There are activists in Japan from Uyghur who receive threatening calls from mainland China, saying that their brother or mother has been thrown into an internment camp. This is a clear violation of national sovereignty. Even if you come from a foreign country, as long as you are within Japanese borders, you have the right to free political activity, free speech, and free press, regardless of your religious faith. We have been very angered by things like this that have happened.

We have asked the people from the Uyghur regions in Japan why they haven't gone to Muslim mosques such as the one in Shibuya to ask for their help. They told us that many spies from mainland China come to Muslim mosques, making it difficult for them to go there. It surprised me to find that things like this have been happening. We haven't heard any Muslim country voice criticism regarding such things before, but Turkey has recently expressed their disavowal.*

The reason why an activist from Uyghur has come to us is because they haven't received any help from Prime Minister Abe even though they have been repeatedly requesting for his aid over several years. He said that he came to us because there was no one else but me they could turn to. Hearing this, I could only feel obliged to help. Perhaps it's a bit odd to be expressing my thoughts on behalf of followers of Islam, but we have told the United Nations about my opinions. I have also talked about them in Germany and now, I'm talking about them here, in Taiwan.

Righteousness is the basis on which I think about things because I feel that everyone should build their future upon what is righteous. This is the message I came here to give to you, the people of Taiwan, and these are the things that Mr. Xi Jinping definitely didn't want me to talk about.

I've now told you what I came here to say. The rest falls upon yourselves to choose the future you wish to see. Japan will do as much as it can. You can put your trust in that. But the future you choose to build will depend on each of you, or it may depend on the outcome of combining your strengths. It's not my intention to bind you to any outcome, but please do remember that you have friends.

---

[*] The Turkish government released a statement on February 9, 2019 criticizing the Chinese government and calling to close its internment (reeducation) camps in the Xinjiang Uyghur region.

Japan has formed diplomatic ties with the most number of countries around the world, so by building ties with Japan, you will be building ties with the rest of the world. Taiwan's foreign ties have decreased, and this has been a problem for your country. When I came here eleven years ago, your country had diplomatic relations with twenty-three countries. But this number has shrunken more and more (seventeen countries as of March 2019) as a result of "salami slicing." This is a sign of the severe circumstances that may ultimately be awaiting you.

So, I ask you not to look at Taiwan's relationship with Japan through your hatred and other emotions of the past. Please try to overcome them and use this relationship to bring about a constructive future. I will be glad if we can do this. To add one more word, I hope you will lend your ears to the voices of the activists living in the PRC and in North Korea who are seeking to bring freedom and happiness to their people.

The Future that Taiwan and China Should Aim to Create

Q1

Through measures of all kinds, Beijing is pressuring other countries to acknowledge its territorial claims on Taiwan, which has brought anger to us, Taiwanese people, the more that they've done so. The Chinese philosopher, Confucius, has taught that word will spread about a government that brings its people happiness and will attract people of other countries to it, but I feel this teaching has been forgotten by the Beijing administration. How would you advise the Chinese leaders who insist on Taiwan's integration into China? Can you also give your advice to the candidates of the 2020 presidential election in Taiwan?

Why Taiwan's integration into China is unrighteous

RYUHO OKAWA

Beijing insists that they should integrate Taiwan because they have the same ethnicity. But in Europe, the people of Sweden and Germany also share Germanic origins, but no one has ever said that they are the same countries. This example alone shows that having the same ethnicity isn't a reason for unifying two countries.

Furthermore, Taiwan's independence came as a result of Japan's defeat in World War II. It was, in particular, an outcome of Japan's defeat against the United States. Chiang Kai-shek's Republic of China was admitted by the Allied Powers as an ally when this occurred and it became a permanent member of the United Nations Security Council. We can, therefore, say that it was the Republic of China, not the People's Republic of China (PRC), that had gained independence. Then (in 1949), four years after Japan's defeat, there was a civil war in which Mao Zedong won. This drove Chiang Kai-shek to flee to Taiwan, splitting the country into two.

The right perspective based on history, then, is to say that the PRC had usurped the land that originally belonged to the Republic of China. This was what had historically occurred and no other explanation is possible. In other words, since it was the land belonging to the Republic of China that was seized by the PRC, the PRC cannot demand for territory to be returned to them, since none of it had ever belonged to them in the first place. A huge portion of land belonging to the Republic of China was taken by the Communist Party of China, leaving them to make do with what territory they possessed in Taiwan. The PRC is now trying to seize even this final footing and telling Taiwan, "give it back to us," but this is very greedy of them to say.

Beijing's promise of allowing the "one country, two systems" policy in Hong Kong was a lie

If the PRC were a good country and an integration would bring happiness to the Taiwanese people, this isn't something I would be against doing; this is one idea that could be considered if that happens to be the case. Since history moves fluidly, if a larger and greater country that brings happiness to their people will result by a unification with China, I would also be in support of such an idea. However, their "Great Chinese Empire" has virtually formed into a totalitarian state, as I mentioned earlier, and Taiwan's integration would undermine your nation of the most important institutions of basic human rights—the principle of democracy, a system of freedom, and faith—that you established over the course of many decades.

Of course, the PRC may talk about the "one country, two systems" policy which will allow a region belonging to their country to follow a separate system. But they have already broken their promise of permitting this system in Hong Kong. After the handover from British rule, Hong Kong was guaranteed 50 years of continued freedom and prosperity (the institutions that were followed during

British occupation) under the "one country, two systems" principle. But in less than 10 years since this handover, Hong Kong already began to lose their freedom, and they will tell you about their growing impoverishment if you ask them. This shows that the PRC had other ideas, and their true intentions were elsewhere.

Should Taiwan be approached with this "one country, two systems" policy, you should tell the PRC to please show you this system being actually implemented in Hong Kong. If they can do this, this will show that you will probably be safe for at least 50 years, and the PRC should be able to make you an offer like that. But they clearly haven't kept their word to Hong Kong, at present. Something is wrong about this that tells us Beijing is lying to the world and you will need to say that to them in clear terms.

Why there is no reason to fear the PRC's military capabilities

Because of the PRC's large population, large economic activity, and huge military power, you may fear them, but you do not need to at this time. Ever since President Trump took office, the United States has drastically changed their policy. Since last fall (in 2018), a dozen U.S. strategic bombers, capable of flying at and sending bombs from an altitude of 15,000 meters (9 miles), have been deployed to the island of Guam. On the other hand, the PRC holds Russian-made anti-aircraft missiles, but which are only capable of reaching just short of 10,000 meters (6 miles) high. Therefore, a system to launch attacks without suffering attacks by the enemy has been already put in place by the United States, and since last fall, all the targets of this system have been focused on Beijing. Should the United States get serious with Beijing, it is bound to face helplessness. Dealing with the North Korean issue is but a non-issue and simply child's play to the U.S., and its decision to take serious action will lead to an attack like the one on Beijing which I have just described.

What's more, the PRC's missiles for sinking the aircraft carriers in the U.S. Seventh Fleet are designed to launch from locations in mainland China, not their naval forces, while missiles for striking these intermediate-range missile sites are being manufactured in Japan. Meaning, Japan has prepared preventative measures to thwart the PRC's attacks on U.S. aircraft carriers, giving you little need to worry about the military issue. What's most important is that your heart remains unshaken.

The PRC should build a true parliamentary system

I wish for the opinions of people in Hong Kong to be taken in as much as possible, and for a political party in mainland China to be established based on ideas practiced by Taiwan and Hong Kong, so that a system of at least two major political parties can be set up in the PRC. Aside from the existing Communist Party of China, another party called the "Party for the Freedom of China," for example, can be created, allowing for debates over political policies to be carried out, and for a true parliamentary system to be established. You all have the right to insist on this and tell them, "We don't need to become integrated if doing so won't lead to our happiness."

The Kind of Country that Brings People Happiness

Q2

You said, eleven years ago, that a unification won't necessarily bring us justice, bring us good, or be the best thing to do, and what's more important is for our people to live in happiness. How do you define this happiness you told us about?

The people in a democracy are not the means, but the purpose

RYUHO OKAWA

Philosophers and politicians of many kinds in search of ways to bring their people happiness have appeared and worked actively to do so. Continuing what I have said earlier on achieving this, the democratic system considers each and every person as not the means, but the purpose. In other words, underlying democracy is the idea of achieving the happiness of each person, not using each person as a means in achieving the country's aims, and this is the purpose of the political, economic, and other forms of cultural activities. Contrary to this, a totalitarian system does not hesitate to jeopardize their people for the sake of national reputation, honor, dignity, and prestige. Countries like this have occurred many times throughout history when feudal governments and monarchical rule by malevolent kings emerged, bringing long periods of such a type of rule.

Looking at Thailand as an example, I made the decision for the third time this January (2019) to cancel my lecture there. Even though they have shown dislike and criticism toward communism, I haven't been able to go there because of the monarchical system of government in their country. The king of Thailand is revered as a god-like being, making it forbidden to defame him. Doing so, as well as criticizing Thailand's system of government, is forbidden not only within but also beyond Thailand's borders. Those who do so will be arrested the moment they set foot inside their country's borders.

Monarchical rule like this is being practiced even in a country that is seen to criticize communism. Even when political parties and a parliament exist, political decisions are powerless against the military when complete control over the military is held by the king and mobilization depends on his approval. Thailand may appear to take the form of a democracy, but they don't behave as one, and this anti-communist country, even now, is being run by a government unfortunately still resembling an autocratic system of rule.

Communism only brought about the equality of impoverishment

Considering these things, the concept that the "sovereignty lies with the people" is, overall, a very revolutionary way of thinking and this idea should, in essence, be compatible with the ideal communism. This may be hard to understand, but both concepts are supposed to be in agreement with each other, because the original idea of communism was to unite the proletariat—the working class—of all countries, and bring down capitalists who are exploiting them, in order that the working class can govern themselves and build their country into a new utopian world.

This is not what communism achieved, however, and instead, it succeeded in giving equal impoverishment, not equal wealth, to everyone. To produce wealth, we need to allow people who use their own ingenuity, effort, perspiration, and hard work into producing better work than others to achieve wealth. Wealth cannot be created unless we do so. The system of communism works, instead, as a principle of jealousy toward those who produce large wealth or build their own business through much harder work than others. Businesses and fortunes created through hard work are seen by communism as unjust, and that they should all be redistributed to other people.

This clear rationalization of jealousy is an issue even though the original idea underlying communism had started with good intentions. Under a system that allows jealousy to hinder those who succeed through perseverance, a country cannot prosper, and everyone will have to live in a state of equal impoverishment.

Only a Japanization can open up the future of China

Everyone should be equal under communism. But the communist party of the PRC has 90 million members—around 6 percent of their population—who hold a social standing equal to the Japanese samurai class of the past. It's beneath this class where there are people profiting through commercial businesses who are invited to become leaders of the communist party. The industrial working class are below them, followed by the farming class, and then those who are too poor to feed themselves. This wealth gap in mainland China is actually growing very large, much larger than it is in Japan. By contrast, Japan is the first country in the world, in fact, to actualize the equality of wealth among its people even though it has not been a communist country.

The Great Leap Forward policy and the Cultural Revolution in the PRC brought tens of millions of their people to their deaths, so after Mao Zedong, Deng Xiaoping prevented the PRC from collapsing the way that the Soviet Union had by reforming and opening up the PRC's economy, saying that it doesn't matter whether a cat is black or is white; it is a good cat if it catches mice, and whoever can make an earning should do so. This implemented a new approach into their system. But even this approach has now come to a deadlock in the PRC. The collapse of the bubble economy like the one once experienced in Japan has already begun there.

Because bureaucrats or governmental officials developing their country's plans are unable to tell the actual results of implementing their plans across the country, a state-led planned economy can only lead to failure. The regional government will definitely report back the numbers set by the central government, making it seem as if they've achieved their goals. But this won't be the reality, and the central government will never realize this. A pattern similar to this and the subsequent collapse of the bubble economy has been experienced already by Japan.

And although Japan didn't implement communism, its social welfare adapts a system that redistributes wealth, so any impoverished person in need of help can receive a certain level of support for their basic needs. Japan redistributes its wealth in this way, and basically, even a company president can earn only about 10 times that of a new staff, although I believe that some outstanding executives deserve to earn more. Assets of tens to hundreds of billions of yen are owned by a minority of the privileged political class in mainland China, but this will never be possible in Japan.

Japan, though not a communist country, has already realized a part of the ideal of communism. If the PRC wishes to open up its future, the only way to do so is through Japanization. The issue will be whether the PRC will realize this. The PRC will eventually realize that the happiness brought about by free trade isn't possible through placing pressure on other countries through military expansion.

Japan will wage a financial war with the Chinese government*, in due time. I have already said my opinion about this, so Japan will take action in due course. There will be a race to test which of the two, Tokyo or Beijing, can set up a more successful capitalist system based on financial strength. Since Beijing unfortunately lacks understanding of how capitalism works, I believe that Japan will come out as the winner. You will see this coming about in a few years' time. We, at Happy Science, have already envisioned the realization of such a future design, and we know that the future will head in this direction.

---

*In the "Spiritual Interview with the Guardian Spirit of Haruhiko Kuroda, Governor of the Bank of Japan" recorded on February 17, 2019, the guardian spirit of Governor Kuroda indicated that Japan could possibly wage a financial war on China.

Creating a society that sees next year will be better than this one

A society in which every person is able to sense and say that, this year has been better than last year, and the next year will be better than this one, is what happiness is. In contrast, happiness can't be found in a country like North Korea where their leader is the only happy person, or in a country like Communist China where only the elite class is able to earn much money, hold power, and send people who oppose them to concentration camps or purge them. The heart that places importance on cherishing each individual is vital.

Mr. Lee Teng-hui said that the "one country, two systems" policy cannot be trusted without democracy, freedom, and fairness in the PRC, and that it's unthinkable for Taiwan to ever be integrated by the Beijing government. What does this fairness mean? It is the acknowledgement, to a certain degree, of an individual's ingenuity and effort that is put into a person's achievement, which the principle of capitalism offers.

By emphasizing the pursuit of equal results, everyone would stop working because they will be treated the same however much they work. This is what will result in such a society, and this needs to be overcome. The essential principles are known already throughout the world. The issue is how you will go about choosing to follow and learning them. Taiwanese people, in large number, may learn new languages when studying abroad, but they won't be able to learn ideas and philosophies that are important to their future. Only the body of teachings and books from Happy Science can offer these things to them. The world is beginning to acknowledge this.

I have published more than 2,500 books, and given more than 2,900 lectures. Around the world there are hundreds of millions of people reading my books. The world is heading in the direction I have shown you to. Though slowly, the world is certain to move in the direction I have discussed. In the 22nd century, you shall see that my words have become general knowledge. Thank you. *Zaijian!* ("Good-bye!" in Chinese.)

Further Reading

What is True Democracy?

Excerpt from
"The Realization of Buddhaland Utopia"

Lecture given on November 9, 2008
at Taipei Local Temple, Happy Science
Taipei, Taiwan

1
Freedom of Religion is
the Basis for Democracy

The spreading of Happy Science philosophies in China means that ultimately, the Chinese government will have to recognize the freedom of religion. Democracy is founded based on the freedom of religion, freedom of faith. Without it, democracy really wouldn't work. If you regard people as objects or as machines, basically, they will be as valueless as dirt and stones, and the nobility of humankind will be lost. However, humans are precious for the very reason that they are the children of God or Buddha. That is the true meaning of human rights in democracy. Because humans are the children of God or Buddha, they are precious and their rights must be valued.

Recognizing religious freedom means recognizing the freedom to believe in God or Buddha, which is the freedom of the mind. This freedom to think as you like in your mind is the starting point of human rights. This is a much more important and fundamental right than the freedom to express political opinions. It is very difficult to live your life if the thoughts in your mind are constrained by other people. So, the freedom of religion comes first, followed by the freedom of speech and the freedom of press. Democracy is always accompanied by the freedom of speech and press, but the freedom of religion precedes them. From the freedom of religion comes the freedom to profess your faith, then the freedom of expression such as speech and press. This is the process, so it is an extremely important point, the starting point, for democracy to recognize the freedom of faith.

This is not just my own opinion. The famous German sociologist Max Weber, who wrote books such as *The Protestant Ethic and the Spirit of Capitalism* and *Ancient Judaism*, also said that religion flourishes in an age of democracy. Democracy accepts different values and ways of thinking. That is why various religions flourish and grow. He said that many religions emerge and flourish through constructive competition over how to make people happy. So, the world-famous German scholar thought democracy and religion were compatible. I dare cite this as one of the grounds for my argument.

2

Why is Democracy the Best System?

I would like to make another point regarding democracy. More than 30 years ago (from the time of this lecture), I majored in law and political science at the University of Tokyo, Faculty of Law. However, even though I studied political science in school, I wasn't convinced as to why democracy was the best system. If you read ancient Greek philosophy by people like Socrates and Plato, democracy was regarded as a low-level system. If the people are ignorant, there is a high risk that democracy will quickly turn into mobocracy and they will easily be ruled by a dictator. So, ancient Greek philosophers did not highly evaluate democracy. In fact, Socrates was put on trial in the Athenian People's Court in 399 B.C. and was sentenced to death, so his disciple Plato hated democracy. With that in my head, when I was a student, I couldn't find an answer as to why democracy was best.

But after graduation, as I read many books, I found the answer in the words of Konosuke Matsushita, the founder of Panasonic. After World War II, he went on a trip to America for the first time. He had observed America for himself and concluded that he understood that democracy was the doctrine of prosperity. When I came across those words, I clearly understood why democracy was best. Konosuke Matsushita hadn't studied political science in school, but when he went to see America as an entrepreneur, he saw various industries flourishing under democracy. The economy flourishes because individuals all use their brain, work hard and do their best to improve their company. He stated clearly that democracy is the doctrine of prosperity. These words show his enlightenment.

In contrast, socialism is a system where some bureaucrats or officials of the central government control the country. But since they can't monitor everything, what occurs is a planned economy where people cannot work to their true potential. In a democracy, people come up with their own ideas and they work to make their company the best it can be, which is how America prospered. No matter how many books by political scientists I've read, I couldn't understand why democracy was the best, but the meaning clicked when I read the words of Konosuke Matsushita, the man who actually built a huge company of tens of thousands of employees in a single generation, without having completed elementary school. In short, a society will grow and flourish more through the combined wisdom of many people, rather than the wisdom of a single person. This is where democracy is excellent.

Let me repeat the two things I have said concerning democracy. One important point about democracy is that religion flourishes in an age of democracy because it allows people to have different ways of thinking and value systems. That's why an age of religion and an age of democracy are compatible. An age when religion is suppressed is not an age of true democracy; therefore, even if a country calls itself "democratic," it's not true democracy if it suppresses all religion. Religion and democracy go together. They prosper together.

Another important point is that democracy is valuable because it is the doctrine of prosperity. In other words, a truly democratic state or society will prosper economically and the people there will become wealthy in both the material and mental sense. That is democracy. We can say that this kind of democracy is the most highly developed form of government.

3

It is More Important for People to Live Happily than to Create a Unified Nation

Seen from that perspective, I think Taiwan is a country where democracy is applied in the truest sense and is prospering greatly. Therefore, a unification is not desirable if it takes away the prosperity you have now. It would be better not to unify your country hastily with a country under a system that does not recognize religious freedom or does not allow growth and prosperity through individual effort.

The unification of a country is not always the best thing. For example, was the unification under Qin Shi Huang a good thing? Insurrection broke out all around, and the situation was dire under an oppressive state. There is always oppression when trying to unify a state. Was Napoleon's rule of Europe good? It did cause many people to suffer. There was also an age when Mongols ruled China and created a unified nation, the Yuan Dynasty. The Yuan Dynasty became the greatest state in the world and, historically speaking, that may have been a great accomplishment. But a huge number of people died in the process.

So, we cannot say that it is always right, good, or best to unify a country. The important thing is to build a society where the inhabitants can live truly happily, while opening up a path through their own efforts. You must know that the nation comes second to that. The best thing is for the people living in a place to be happy. If they are, the structure of the country doesn't really matter.

4
The Criterion to Discern between Good Nations and Bad Nations

All countries claim that they are good, but there is a simple criterion for judging which countries are good and which are bad. A country where many people want to defect or emigrate to is a good country. A country where many people flee from is a bad country. It's a very simple way to judge. A country where many foreigners want to go to and live in is a good one, whereas a country that many people want to flee from is a bad one.

Based on this standard, let us compare, for example, America and the Soviet Union— the two countries that fought a lengthy Cold War after World War II. Many people from many different places traveled to America to study or work, and some of them went back and worked hard to develop their own country. In contrast, not many people fled to the Soviet Union. In this way, you can judge for yourself whether a country is good or bad.

PART II

SPIRITUAL INTERVIEW

In Part II, there are a total of eight interviewers, abbreviated as S, A, I, O, R, M, C, and K, in the order that they first appear.

Spiritual Interview with the Guardian Spirit of Xi Jinping (Excerpt)

Recorded on June 21, 2018
at Special Lecture Hall, Happy Science
Tokyo, Japan

1
"Dictatorships are Strong, Democracies are Weak"

"My time has finally come"

XI JINPING'S GUARDIAN SPIRIT:
Ahh, hmm...

S:
Are you the guardian spirit of Xi Jinping, President of the People's Republic of China?

XI'S G.S.:
Yes, that's right.

S:
I'd like to thank you for providing this opportunity to interview you for the first time in six years[*].

---

[*]Okawa previously recorded spiritual interviews with the guardian spirit of Xi Jinping in October 2010 and September 2012. See *Sekai Kotei wo Mezasu Otoko* (lit. "The Man Aiming to Become the World Emperor") (Tokyo: Happiness Realization Party, 2010) and *China's Hidden Agenda: The Mastermind Behind the Anti-American and Anti-Japanese Protests* (Tokyo: HS Press, 2012).

XI'S G.S.:

Well, thanks to you guys, it's been revealed that I am the reincarnation of Genghis Khan[†], and I look more charismatic, which was very helpful in my seizing power.

S:

In a sense, we are very proud that Happy Science was the first to point out President Xi's true power, and we were the ones to release the information to the rest of the world.

XI'S G.S.:

Yes, you must be proud. Thanks to you, we were able to make good progress in taking control of Mongolia. The fact that I've accomplished the feat of becoming "president for life," something that hadn't been done since Mao Zedong, means my time has finally come. Hahaha...

S:

I deeply admire your ability to establish this power base over the past six years.

[†] According to spiritual research conducted by Happy Science, Xi Jinping was likely born as Genghis Khan in his past life. Genghis Khan was the first emperor of the Mongol Empire. See the aforementioned *Sekai Kotei wo Mezasu Otoko*.

XI'S G.S.:

Contrary to expectations, I have a strategic mind. That's why when I was vice president, there was no precedent at the time and I don't recall who approached whom, but I visited Japan and had an audience with that emperor of Heisei*, the era which will end soon. Until then he normally would only meet the president, but I gave a warning to the people of Japan that our meeting while I was still only the vice president indicated that I would eventually become someone in a much higher position in the future.

S:

I see. It may have indicated a warning, but I was very impressed that you nonchalantly met the emperor on short notice. At the time, there were talks that Ichiro Ozawa† helped make the meeting happen. We've seen events like this in the past, but today, it seems like we're entering an age where the state and the history of the world are beginning to change significantly.

---

*Xi Jinping visited Emperor Akihito of Japan in December 2009 during his term as the vice president of China. It was an unprecedented event; no Chinese vice president had ever met with the Japanese emperor. Furthermore, the Imperial Household Agency had disapproved Xi's wish to see the emperor since the appointment was requested less than one month in advance. Foreign figures usually ask for an appointment with the Japanese emperor more than one month before the desired date. However, the Japanese cabinet and other politicians at the time worked to make this happen, and the meeting was held. Some Japanese people saw this as "using the emperor for a political purpose." In Japan, the emperor must not be "used" for any political purpose.

† Ichiro Ozawa (1942–present) is a Japanese politician who formerly served as a secretary-general of the Democratic Party of Japan when Xi visited Japan.

As you know, the North Korea–United States Summit was held on June 12 (2018), and after that Kim Jong-un, the Chairman of the Workers' Party of Korea, visited Beijing to greet and maybe report the result to President Xi Jinping. I would love to know before the rest of the world how you view this sequence of events and what your next step will be.

XI'S G.S.:
What percentage of the truth should I disclose?

S:
Oh, 100 percent. We would appreciate 120 percent.

XI'S G.S.:
Really? I mean, you are quite a sly fox, aren't you?

S:
No, no, not at all.

XI'S G.S.:
It won't be good to get tricked into saying too much. Don't you know that a slip of the tongue is what leads to a downfall? I need to be careful of what I say.

S:

Well, I don't think you're in a position anymore where you have to worry about losing power.

XI'S G.S.:

Even with my power, I can't purge you guys as long as you are living in Japan. If you ever come to Beijing, I can have you guys arrested.

Each side achieved half their goals at the North Korea–United States Summit

S:

Needless to say, we are not expecting any slips of the tongue. Understanding how this situation is viewed from the perspective of a great politician such as yourself will serve as material for people throughout the world to study, so we would love to hear your candid opinions.

XI'S G.S.:

Yes, I understand.

S:

So first, the North Korea–United States Summit was held on June 12. As explained by Master Okawa in the beginning, there have been various reactions from the American and Japanese media as well as politicians that it is difficult to tell whether the North Korea–

United States Summit accomplished any results. Among them, there have been people who believe that Kim Jong-un achieved a runaway victory, but the current situation is that we still don't know for sure who came out on top.

Based on information from the spiritual world, we have learned that President Trump managed to get Chairman Kim Jong-un to commit to the denuclearization and the bloodless surrender of Pyongyang, which resulted in the development of a sweeping trend. How do you view this situation?

XI'S G.S.:

I think that both countries have achieved half their goals. For one, I think that things will continue to progress according to those words. However, another thing is that the leader of a small nation North Korea which recently set off those "fireworks" had a meeting on equal terms, in Singapore, with the president of a superpower like the United States.

And then there is the fact that Kim Jong-un made "pilgrimage" to Beijing. If you can't understand the meaning behind this, I don't know what else to say.

S:

I see. So, you mean to say, one key point is that a small nation North Korea held discussions with a major powerhouse like the United States on equal terms. And the other point is that Chairman Kim Jong-un then immediately went to report the results of the summit to President Xi Jinping. You said it is important to understand the meaning behind these. So, what exactly is the meaning behind these?

XI'S G.S.:

It means that it's no longer an age when the United States and China have talks as a way of hegemonic war. It is now a time when North Korea and the United States can negotiate on equal footing. And that means that the Beijing government, in other words, the People's Republic of China which possesses the power of life and death over North Korea, has become a "super-super" superpower that has exceeded both North Korea and the United States.

S:

In a sense, it looks like you're in a position to make up the rules and control the game in which these two players are competing against each other...

XI'S G.S.:

Hmm, well, more like a referee. We're the ones who blow the whistle on a foul and raise the flag.

S:

So, you mean, you're now in that position?

XI'S G.S.:

Yes.

North Korea is merely "a province of China"

S:

As the premise of those words, you said that they were half right and that things would continue to proceed as they are. Can you explain in detail what you meant? We see the denuclearization, guarantee of the current regime and opening-up of the economic problems among others of North Korea, and furthermore the democratization and liberalization of the country down the line. Do you think so, too?

XI'S G.S.:

The thing is, you guys overestimate him (Kim Jong-un) and think that North Korea is a nation, but from my point of view, North Korea is merely "a province of China." Do you understand? A province... Well, to put it in a way that you can better relate, I'd say that Kim Jong-un is to our government what the governor of Iwate is to the government of Japan.

To be honest, to us, it's like, whether to remove nuclear facilities from Iwate Prefecture, or to remove the missile launch bases; whether or not to provide assistance, supply food, or build houses if the people of Iwate Prefecture are struck by a disaster. We recognize differently from you. You may think of them as a nation, but from our point of view, they're just one of our many provinces. It seems like North Korea has the capacity to shoot a maximum of 60 missiles, but realistically that figure is probably closer to 20 missiles. They possess ballistic missiles that could be equipped with nuclear warheads, but to us, it's all the same whether we move those weapons to some other province of China. Or, we could just develop and increase our weapons there. Ultimately, our capability won't change. It's just our annexed province. So basically, we are not affected by them whatsoever.

S:

From your perspective, do you believe that it is disgraceful or weak of the United States, the world's strongest democracy, to panic over 20 or so nuclear missiles?

XI'S G.S.:

Yes. You know, they (North Korea) were able to deal with the United States on equal terms. President Trump really did show up brazenly, going as far as Singapore... He arrived with probably around 100 bodyguards, but after seeing him get scared simply because of the presence of nuclear weapons and holding negotiations with that cheap gangster's tiny country on equal terms, I realized that they are no longer an enemy to us.

Letting the media run loose is what weakens the country

S:

So, what we saw was a weakness of democracy...

XI'S G.S.:

They are weak. I've truly realized how letting the media run loose can weaken a country this much. Ha. I've come to firmly understand that dictatorial-autocratic-totalitarian states are indeed more than ten times as strong as democratic states.

S:

Of course, in democratic states, the mass media write whatever they want. But in a democracy, the life of each and every citizen is cherished. Is that type of thinking becoming a weakness for them?

XI'S G.S.:

You basically believe that opposing those in power brings happiness to the people, right? Even we know that. But it is only good in preventing a dictatorship. When dealing with a country like us who are actively developing its dictatorship, or a country like North Korea which is basically already a dictatorship, they are forced to be on equal terms even when there is an overwhelming difference in strength between the two parties.

Even when it came to pushing the nuclear missile button, Trump would never be actually be able to go through with it. Unless he is able to obtain all the consent that is required, there's no way he would be able to push that button. However, in Kim's case, if he ever feels annoyed after eating dinner, he could act alone and launch all the missiles he wants. How crazy... And on top of that the media never criticize him, and everyone will say, "that's wonderful," right?

If they don't say that, they will be beheaded by the next day. How crazy... That's why I've come to realize that we possess over ten times their strength.

2

The Outlook of the U.S.-China Trade War

"The U.S. is not in a position to fight"

S:

We just heard an extremely important way of thinking right now. Actually putting efforts on the Korean Peninsula means that the power of the United States and Japan will be greatly diverted, and as a result, that will benefit China. I would like to ask you from a different point of view, but some of the experts' ideas on Japanese national defense said that, with the withdrawal of U.S. forces from South Korea, they have already begun to shift to issues against China, such as the South China Sea issue. In other words, there are also people who say so as a result of observing the movements of the United States Secretary of Defense Jim Mattis who has resolved the North Korean problem and now started to take action by seeing China as the main threat, as well as the appointment of the United States Ambassador to South Korea Harry B. Harris, Jr. There are views that China is probably on the receiving end of the target from the U.S. What do you think about these?

XI'S G.S.:

Hahaha [*laughs*]. Too bad. Really, too bad. Those military folks you expect so much from have no idea about economy at all, so they really don't realize that the United States is not in a position to fight. Yes, it's really too bad. President Trump is in a position where he has to really economize to live. His budget is tight. Military men only know how to spend, so they aren't thinking like that. President Trump is trying hard to create jobs for the population and create income for those who do not have income, but is not really keen on spending taxes for war. So in fact, his regime is much less of a threat than the Democratic Party. In a sense, he can't fight because he has too much management sense.

A:

So that means, he actually has a stronger sense of a battle on economic terms right?

XI'S G.S.:

But President Trump doesn't have much experience with trade either. All he's done was to buy and sell land in the U.S. He has no understanding of trade, he is not an international businessman.

S:

However, there is still this unknown factor as to how much President Xi has an understanding of the trade war and such.

XI'S G.S.:

As a real estate agent, definitely above Trump. Because I have intentions of taking Europe which is just across the land from us [*laughs*]. Hmm. It's going to get big. Because I'm thinking about stomping on Russia as well if Putin ever trips.

"China can cause a great depression in the U.S."

A:

However, with the trade sanction President Trump is taking to reduce China's trade surplus with the U.S., wouldn't the flow of China's funds dry out if this continues for one year, two years or...

XI'S G.S.:

That's what people will think, right? However, Chinese people spend their money in Japan to buy a lot, right? If you go to the U.S. like New York, there are crowds of Chinese buying stuff there. When all this disappears like receding waves, will the U.S. economy get better? I mean, just compare our population.

A:

The U.S. is increasing employment by about 3 million people per year, so I think, in a sense, China will have less effect.

XI'S G.S.:

No, the Chinese tourists will disappear so they will not buy anything. And the United States will strive to make their citizens rich. And all the surrounding countries will block the U.S. economy and the United States will become isolated. And Monroe Doctrine* will start. Like something we saw in the past, right? Next, the United States will say, "We don't want to get involved in any war." When they become isolated economically they will next not be involved in any war whatsoever. And they will say "Conflicts? Well Japan, solve them yourselves."

S:

However, looking at the trade between the United States and China, I would think it will cause harm to China if the trade with the United States becomes stagnant. Because what supports the Chinese economy is what they earn from exports. The domestic demand of the Chinese will not increase as is.

XI'S G.S.:

But you see, if we want to cause a depression in the U.S., it would be a piece of cake. China owns the most number of U.S. government bonds. If we sold them all off, then the United States will instantly go into a great depression. So, a conflict does not just mean a war. We can cause a war economically as well.

---

*The Monroe Doctrine was a foreign policy conducted by the fifth U.S. President James Monroe (served 1817–1825). It advocated non-interference between Europe and the U.S., and is also called isolationism.

S:

Yes. I see, I guess we can see this as China using U.S. government bonds as a shield or a hostage.

XI'S G.S.:

If we sold them off, that will cause a great depression. In an instant, all those elite businessmen on Wall Street will become unemployed. So, the farmers and miners may be joyful that they have been given jobs but in rusted...Rust Belt, is it?

S:

It's Rust Belt.

XI'S G.S.:

It may be that in rusty industrial areas employment has recovered somewhat, but will the United States hold if Wall Street becomes storm of the unemployed?

S:

However, there is another point of view. If the U.S. government bonds are sold and the value of the U.S. government bonds plummets, the dollar will also collapse at the same time, and that will also be devastating to China who is preparing foreign currency centered on the U.S. dollar.

XI'S G.S.:

But, hey, America is a country of individualism. China is, after all, a country of totalitarianism. By saying that it is in a state of war, and telling Chinese people to endure, everyone will endure it. All they have to do is endure and eat sorghum.

Well, Japan is in a riskier state. If the United States is pushed to that extent, then Japan will be next and Japan will crumble quickly. That will be quite serious. Now a country with a debt of 1,100 trillion yen, if the U.S. economy (crisis) came again, Japan will instantly become a heavy debtor and become like Argentina. That would be devastating, too.

"World history will be dominated by Chinese rule"

A:

But when we look at the situation of the economy right now, I think the most unstable is China.

XI'S G.S.:

No, China is doing very well. Because we are actually an agricultural nation. If something happens, we can all return to working in agriculture. So, there's no problem at all.

A:

I guess if that's the case there is nothing to worry about [*laughs*], but regarding modern issues, there was the collapse of stocks centered on Shanghai and then the collapse of the land bubble, so aren't you bearing it by force? Thus, the most unstable country is China, and I feel it will become something like a game of chicken with the United States.

XI'S G.S.:

But with the One Belt One Road Initiative, we are now ready to take the EU and Africa as well. The "Century of China" is starting. You will see the future world of a single-state domination by China. Hmm.

S:

I see. Because I want to ask you about various opinions you have, I will dare debate against you. That said, it is actually a fact that you are trying to guarantee the Chinese Yuan by pegging (applying fixed exchange rate) it to the dollar to protect its value, aren't you? As a matter of fact, if the United States became serious about China's liberalization of finance or tried to encourage it to China with the IMF (International Monetary Fund) etc., the Chinese Yuan will crash and have devastating effects on the Chinese economy. There is an opinion that this is a very scary vulnerable point for the Chinese economy. What is your view on this pressure against finance liberalization?

XI'S G.S.:

No worries as Taiwan, South Korea, and Japan will be paying "land tax."

S:

Land tax? Oh.

XI'S G.S.:

Because it will be a necessary tribute. Indeed. What they have created until now, we will commandeer. Yes.

S:

Then, just like a former gunboat diplomacy, you can threaten Japan, Korea or Taiwan backed by your mighty military force, and force promotion of investment in China...

XI'S G.S.:

Even Japanese department stores will surely be shocked if they hear Chinese tourists will not come anymore. Prime Minister Abe's consumption tax (tax increase) itself will be a Japan-killer. Absolutely.

S:

Well, it will be a blow for those that are only expecting inbound sales.

President Trump will reduce military budget as the threat of North Korea decreases

S:

However, as we are talking about various things in detail, in actuality, when we last talked to you, President Xi Jinping's guardian spirit, President Obama was still in office. How are you viewing President Trump?

XI'S G.S.:

Well, he is clearly a Western gunman. So, when he shoots his gun, it's good if he hits, but if he misses, then he will come under fire. Well, that is what it will be.

S:

When compared with President Obama, are there any aspects of President Trump that is easier to handle or harder to handle?

XI'S G.S.:

Well, they are both weak, so there is nothing to be done.

S:

Weak?

XI'S G.S.:

Well, what I mean when I say that there is nothing to be done is that because he's old, he will get weaker year by year. That's President Trump. Obama was relatively young. He had some aspects that were young. And he also was popular internationally, so yeah. Hmm.

S:

In other words, Mr. Trump could do drastic things because he doesn't have time.

XI'S G.S.:

Yes. So, Obama wasn't strong, but he had the sympathy vote, or the power to increase friends. But if President Trump continues to lose friends, he is like "the final Western gunner" and if there are 6 bullets in the chamber and he pulls the trigger to fire all the bullets, then that will be the end.

A:

That is being said by the mass media also, so maybe that is true. But there is another way of viewing it; originally, it was to clean up the North Korean problem during the first term and to confront China during the second term...

XI'S G.S.:

But that is of course, your side of view, right? That is the way of view that suits your side.

A:

However, there is a view that it seems like in just a year and a half, the majority of his work for the first term has been completed, considering that at the North Korea-United States Summit a few days ago, he settled on North Korea for now, and he is heading for China next.

XI'S G.S.:

Well, but hey, Mr. Trump will soon be proud of decreasing the nuclear threat of North Korea. Very soon. Because he will be proud, he will lose focus and the reduction will start. Because the United States will try to reduce their military power and turn toward recovering their national finance. Their military expenses are about the same amount as Japan's general revenue too. It would not get better for them unless they wield this greatly. That's why, thinking that the fear of nuclear war has receded from the world, they will greatly reduce their military expenses. It is of no concern to China, when the enemy starts collapsing all by themselves.

S:

Actually no, though the costs of the U.S. military forces in South Korea and the joint military training of the United States and South Korea will be reduced, we have not heard about the United States reducing other military costs. Although it is fine to be optimistic [*laughs*], the cost will rather continue to increase for China. Military expenses as a defense budget also cost 20 trillion yen annually, and it seems that President Xi Jinping is considering it to be too advantageous for himself.

XI'S G.S.:

Hmm. But before the war between Japan and the United States, the United States was where cars were being built, right? It was a big auto factory for the world. But now, isn't the auto industry being taken over by Toyota, Nissan and others? Yes, it is being taken over. So, in that sense, their main business has already been "devoured," that's the state for them today.

And in Japan, the population is not increasing and only China is a country where the population is expected to increase and is most likely to buy cars. If India was to buy cars, then they have to start out from fixing the roads, not an easy task, and they would have to increase their income a bit more. So, if a breath of fresh air was to be blown into the automobile industry, they would not be able to cut their ties with China. In that sense, hahaha [*laughs*], we are the "savior" and whether they are saved or not is our decision to make.

3

Xi Jinping's Hegemonic Strategy toward 2020

"Taiwan is like a frog competing against an ox"

A:

So, on the premise that China is a savior and now is the era of G1, I would like to ask you about some things. Although it is said that the United States is being drawn into the North Korean problem, there are the south side including Taiwan, the Philippines, Southeast Asia, and then we talked about Malaysia too. How is China planning on ruling these areas around the year 2020?

XI'S G.S.:

Well, we'd like to take it to a state where we can win without fighting as much as we possibly can. It would be a pity to spend money. It would be stupid to actually fight a physical war. We essentially have others perform tribute diplomacy. Taiwan is like a frog competing with an ox. If they can't compete with big China anymore because their stomach has erupted, and gave up, then that would be the end of Taiwan. Well, we will make efforts to prepare the environment, so that it would end that way. Japan has no diplomatic relations with Taiwan anyway. So, there is nothing you can do, right? Hmm.

A:
So, China is creating a situation where the United States cannot intervene...

XI'S G.S.:
Since the United States is also hitting the final jab, they probably will have to pull their fleet out soon. Soon, it will turn into a piston movement between Hawaii and the West Coast. They already have no money. President Trump just recently said that it's tough to launch a long-distance bomber from Guam to North Korea. It costs a lot to do and North Korea is far for them. They don't like that. He said it's not really necessary to go to the other side of the Earth. Well, that's actually true. If you were focusing on rebuilding finance, then that would be absolutely true. There is no need to go to such a place. It's stupid to go to the other side of the Earth and prepare for war. Don't you think so? So, he can concentrate on domestic issues. The United States has now produced "the founder of restoration." Their domestic industry will pick up again, reducing unemployment, and with the Monroe Doctrine, they will isolate themselves from the international community, and will not express their opinion. It's something like that, right?

S:
I think I've just heard a very important strategy right now.

Isolating the United States with
the One Belt One Road Initiative

XI'S G.S.:

China will decide what are human rights issues, and the United States will be criticized based on that*. Well, as China becomes a major world power, and this means that basically earthlings are mostly Chinese, so the Chinese way of thinking about human rights will become the world standard. China will say, "The United States is acting badly by not treating immigrants properly," and everyone will follow up on it.

S:

Surprisingly, I feel like I've heard about President Xi Jinping's vision. Strategically, the economic isolation of the United States due to the trade war, etc., is related to China's One Belt, One Road Initiative, right?

XI'S G.S.:

Well, yes, this is where China differs greatly from the United States. I mean, Mr. Trump is thinking only about his own "house budget." However, we are already trying to put the Chinese belt around the world on a global level. I'm much better in designing a grand plan. There had only been one time when an Eastern country overcame

---

*On June 19, 2018, two days before this spiritual interview, the Trump administration announced the U.S. withdrawal from the UN Human Rights Council.

Europe—during my time (in his past life as Genghis Khan). Every time Japan sends soldiers to the Korean Peninsula, they quickly lose.[†] Europe was occupied only during my era. Hahaha [*laughs*].

S:

Well, in World War II, Japan was quite rampant in China, though. So, your idea is to use the One Belt, One Road Initiative to swiftly take over areas included in it when the United States recedes slightly from the international economy, right?

XI'S G.S.:

Yes. So, the United States is mouthing off a lot on unnecessary matters, such as Iran, but they don't need to worry. The power of the United States will soon wane. All those oil producing countries will all soon fall under our control. The United States can just dig their own shale oil. Then, they will be economically self-sustainable. Because we are sure we're going to get all the desert areas.

S:

Oh, you are?

XI'S G.S.:

Yes, yes. We will take all of them.

[†] After unifying Japan, Hideyoshi Toyotomi (1537–1598), plotting to take over Ming, sent troops against Joseon (Korea) and Ming forces in 1592 and 1597. But in the end, Hideyoshi died in battle and the Japanese forces withdrew after little success.

What is the measure against religious problems?

S:

At that time, how will you deal with this problem with Muslims? In the Islamic world, there is information that the remaining forces of ISIS are going to Uyghur.

XI'S G.S.:

Well, in Uyghur, we are just in the process of instructing them to convert to "Chinese religion" instead of Islam. We will teach them the ideal model ways. So, this large China will probably absorb other countries and become 2 billion and 2.5 billion in population. It will get to a stage where "if you aren't Chinese, you aren't human." Well, we will tell the people in Uyghur how to become an exemplary Chinese.

S:

I see. How do you feel about that from the standpoint of Happy Science International Headquarters, Mr. I?

I:

I believe religion is important. Even if you can physically restrain a person, the mind is a part that cannot be restrained.

XI'S G.S.:

Hmm. If there is a mind, that is.

I:

Now, religion is suppressed quite severely in your country, but what kind of policy do you have about this in the future?

XI'S G.S.:

Well, you can preach the existence of the mind, but it cannot beat food and weapon. Unfortunately, as long as we live on earth. Well, if you stop and take food away, and attack with weapons, then Tibet and Uyghur will be one and the same. Same with Mongolia. You know, it can't be helped. Nothing can be done. Even if your political party says, "Let's liberate Uyghur," it just means to increase the number of people who get killed as a show, so it won't make any sense. You should give up. So, if we have advantage in weapons and control over food, then you can do absolutely nothing even if you preach about the mind.

His strategy against India

I:

Amongst all this, you have a large religious country called India next to you. Do you have any thoughts on strategies against India?

XI'S G.S.:

No problem as we will make Pakistan invade it. I won't do it myself. Pakistan can handle it all by themselves. It should be OK as we will exhaust India by making it compete with Pakistan.

S:

However, the population of India is expected to become the world's largest, even larger than China very soon. Potentially it could be the next threat to China.

XI'S G.S.:

No such thing. The huge population in India indicates that China can potentially gain a large slave class.

S:

You mean India will become China's slave class?

XI'S G.S.:

Oh yes, exactly. It's Shudra. Because we need lower class slaves. China is now moving from middle class to upper class, so that means there will be a lack of lower class labor force. Besides, as aging is slightly progressing, if we can use the strength of growing India as a labor force, well, it's all good.

S:

Maybe you aren't taking seriously the massive religious power of India and the religious power of Christianity.

XI'S G.S.:

Umm, India should be liberated soon. Well, their super-primitive polytheism, like monkey god, cow god, elephant god and such.... it's enough. So, we have to wipe it all out. Well, we do not intent to deny all religions though. In order to make it into a modern religion, I think cleansing it once like what Islam did would be better. In that sense, I think we could temporarily break it down with Marxism or Islam.

"We monitor the lives of all our citizens"

A:
You were talking about suppression of religion and human rights in China, but as long as you are thinking that humans have no mind...

XI'S G.S.:
No, I don't think like that. I am only saying that it cannot win against weapons and food.

A:
Though I can understand your idea, there are many people who are actively faithful to religion and are active underground. So, there are many who will not abandon faith no matter how much they are suppressed.

XI'S G.S.:
But if they were approached with a weapon in the right hand and food in the left hand, they will all go behind iron bars, completely. I do not mind what they fantasize about behind iron bars; they have a

mind, after all. We don't mind if they are delusional since they will not have any effect. OK?

S:

I can understand what you're saying, but now, criticism from international circles is heightening because Liu Xiaobo, who received the Nobel Prize, actually had no other choice but to die while he was ill in jail. And now, his wife cannot freely leave the country, either. These things are gradually leading to an alliance against China.

XI'S G.S.:

Hahaha [*laughs*]. Too naïve. That's why you are all too naïve. What do we care for Liu Xiaobo? He is just a dissident. He is actually just "an ant" compared to a huge nation. Whether they award a Nobel Prize or not, it doesn't have any influence. We easily denied such prestige.

Your democracy is being brainwashed by the mass media. Your democracy is being destroyed by a religion called "mass media." Mr. Trump also. He is losing power because he makes enemies of them. We do not have any media who oppose us and the lives of the people are being monitored by the intelligence police. There is no freedom even in the Internet. Therefore, I think that it is the strongest country right now.

S:

When I first heard you speak eight years ago, you were very thoughtful about the comments you made and I thought you were tough.

XI'S G.S.:

Well, my ability is quite different than what it was then.

S:

On the contrary, I sense that you are a little too confident. I wouldn't usually say such a thing though.

XI'S G.S.:

Well, if you claim to be the reincarnation of Chairman Mao Zedong, then it would be a good competition.

S:

Well from our side, if you are too confident, then that also can become a chance for us as well.

4

Confidence or Arrogance?

Is he underestimating President Trump?

XI'S G.S.:

So, Japan will soon turn from "America's unsinkable aircraft carrier" to "China's unsinkable aircraft carrier." Because we will make the U.S. forces in Japan all withdraw soon. They will be forced to withdraw within a few years.

S:

You will make the U.S. troops in Japan withdraw?

XI'S G.S.:

Yes. This is the beginning, you know? Of course, we will make them withdraw.

S:

So, you mean the change in the situation on the Korean Peninsula is the beginning?

XI'S G.S.:

Well, Taiwan will also fall, and soon.

A:

I think your viewpoint on these are very big thinking and wonderful. On the other hand, the Trump regime gives more attention to the idea that it may be better to have the U.S. troops stationed in Taiwan instead of Japan.

XI'S G.S.:

Well actually, when I look at President Trump I can only see him as the owner of a small grocery store or something like that. Like he owns the store and is trying really hard to buy and sell stuff, something like that... buying and selling second-hand goods? Like he is buying and selling vases and such, that's all I can see him as, an old man.

S:

Well [*smiles wryly*], it might be rude of me to ask you this again, but aren't you underestimating President Trump?

XI'S G.S.:

Again, if you say you are the reincarnation of Chairman Mao Zedong, I will accept your opinion as you will be on equal footing.

S:

[*Laughs.*] OK.

A:

The way you see Mr. Trump is a good thing for us, but even so, it seems to me that you are oblivious to his economic strategy such as the trade war mentioned earlier and military strategy.

XI'S G.S.:

Considering how much attack he is receiving from his country's mass media, he doesn't seem to be such a superior person, does he? He's obese and really just a bit useless? And now, he's immersed in

Judaism, too. He was influenced by his son-in-law and became too involved with Israel, so he made enemies of Arabs. And now the oil-producing countries have to search for other patrons.

S:

No. President Trump has continued to maintain the relationship with Saudi Arabia and Egypt even though he recognized Jerusalem as Israel's capital.

XI'S G.S.:

No, no, no. Because it will be over soon.

S:

Over? How will it end?

XI'S G.S.:

The nations that worship China will have control over their own areas.

Will China be overthrown by religion again?

I:

There's one thing I wanted to ask you about—Europe. Recently, German Chancellor Merkel has approached Japanese Prime Minister Abe, and is slightly changing her policy. On the other hand, Europe is very much dependent on China regarding certain things. Does China have any future strategy against Europe?

XI'S G.S.:

Well, we are thinking about taking it, of course [*laughs*]. That's obvious. That's probably why the U.K. escaped (from the EU). Because if they remained, they also would be taken. The U.K. is trying to escape. Pretty soon, Europe, I mean the EU, will be controlled by China. You might be trying to do world missionary work, but now is your last chance. Since this is the last, you'd better go soon. In a while, you won't be able to go.

I:

I think, even in China, there are more Christian believers than the number of CPC (Communist Party of China) members.

XI'S G.S.:

That's OK. Because all Christians believe in the Communist Party. So, it's perfectly fine. You cannot win against weapons and food. Tibet and Uyghur are all the same. In the end, religion cannot win against weapons and food. That was something Muhammad also indicated. Basically, they cannot win because they cannot win militarily.

A:

However, in the history of China, almost all the regimes have been overthrown by religious forces, right?

XI'S G.S.:

Well, that's history. Today's religions do not have technology. They can just preach the teaching of the mind because it is inexpensive. That's perfectly fine with me.

A:

The Chinese regimes, even in the past, maintained power with the military, but were defeated by religious forces as expected.

XI'S G.S.:

Well, for now we're invincible.

Is Xi Jinping receiving guidance from Qin Shi Huang, who resides in the Spirit World?

S:

Well for me, I wanted to ask you about your recognition on that today. I mean, the Chinese Communist Party Congress held in October of last year (2017) and the revision of the constitution this year (2018) made it possible for the president of the People's Republic of China to be a lifetime position.

XI'S G.S.:

Well, it can't be helped. We're just imitating the West and just making it look good, but in actuality the constitution will be over if I write it over on toilet paper.

S:

Then, do you recognize yourself as being equal to Mao Zedong now?

XI'S G.S.:

No, I've surpassed him.

S:

Surpassed!?

XI'S G.S.:

Hmm. Yes, surpassed. Mao Zedong was afraid of the Japanese army, so he frantically escaped to survive, and when Japan was destroyed, he finally founded a country [*laughs*]. Don't group me with someone like him.

S:

However, in a sense, I think that it shows how Mao Zedong was a realist. Because he sometimes reverted to Japan and spied for Japan to survive. This could be either good or bad, but are you saying President Xi surpassed that?

XI'S G.S.:

Well now, I have control of 1.4 billion Chinese people. So, I'm not scared of anything.

S:

However, for example, as for President Xi's successor, to the surprise of many people, he did not appoint his projected successor as a member of the Politburo Standing Committee, the leadership section. I'm referring to Mr. Hu Chunhua. And President Xi even drove out Mr. Sun Zhengcai from his position for corruption. Is it all right not to prepare a successor?

XI'S G.S.:

Well, I am currently doing research on eternal youth.

S:

Aren't you receiving rather strong influence by Qin Shi Huang, the emperor of Qin dynasty who resides in the Spirit World?

XI'S G.S.:

Really? I don't know, but maybe so. Eternal youth... Well, now Master Ryuho Okawa himself is also saying we should aim to live 120 years. If we aim for 120 years, then I will have 55 more years of imperialism, so I have enough time to take over the world.

I:

Even Qin Shi Huang could not find the elixir of life. And then, Qin Shi Huang died when he consumed mercury thinking it was the elixir of life.

XI'S G.S.:

Well, that was a result of lack of scientific knowledge, but now that China is very advanced in science and technology, I'll be OK.

S:

Today, we are asking Xi Jinping's guardian spirit, but in reality...

XI'S G.S.:

I'm gaining power. I am now increasing my power. I was the vice president several years ago. Then, I became the president and after several years of accomplishments, I was now able to make it seem as though North Korea and the United States were on equal terms. I feel we are 100 times stronger (than the United States). We can do anything with the world. It is all in my hands.

A:

Your level of recognition is quite "incredible." I would like to talk a bit about the Spirit World. Do you talk with Qin Shi Huang?

XI'S G.S.:

Huh? Umm, the People's Republic of China officially regards religion as opium. So, "talking to Qin Shi Huang" is not possible unless a time machine is invented.

A:

We are talking to the guardian spirit (of Xi Jinping), right?

XI'S G.S.:

Oh, yeah that's right. Well, it's fine because in psychiatry, there is supposed to be something called the deep psyche. Deep psyche is what you are talking with. As it is possible in modern medicine, it should be OK, right?

5

Democracy is Coming to an End?

The aim of the "Xi Empire"

S:

In 20th century China, after the Xinhai Revolution, a person named Yuan Shikai* took power. He got really "messed up," which is to say, after he became emperor, he immediately became ill and died. I am wondering if you are considering turning China into the Xi Empire from a Communist Party dictatorship.

XI'S G.S.:

What? Why are you even asking? Isn't that obvious? I can't believe you are asking such a stupid question. Of course, I am doing that. That is what I am after. Dumb question...

---

*Yuan Shikai (1859–1916) was a Chinese military and government official who became the first president of the Republic of China in 1913. He revived imperialism and became the emperor himself, but abandoned it in 1916 as a result of domestic and foreign opposition.

S:

So, in that case, world emperor...

XI'S G.S.:

I am the world emperor.

S:

... of the Xi Jinping Empire?

XI'S G.S.:

Look, I already am the world emperor.

S:

Well, it does seem like you are chipping away at all sorts of power of other political officials of the CPC and have basically surrounded yourself with yes men. Is this essentially a case of you establishing an imperial household for the Xi Jinping Empire, and are we currently watching this process happening?

XI'S G.S.:

Yes. I have absolute confidence that we will never be beaten by a democratic nation. No matter how hard Mr. Trump works, he only has six more years in office (if he is elected for a second term). But if you look at how the mass media is handling him, things are probably very tough for him right now.

S:

Well, yes, there definitely are difficulties with democracy. But communism as well has its own issues, such as the inability to hold personal power, the fact that it is a group leadership system, not to mention the intense antipathy toward worshipping an individual. So, I do feel that even communism has its limits...

XI'S G.S.:

Umm, you know, I have already surpassed communism. Well, I mean, I was born to actualize "super communism," which is to say, to actualize Marx's prediction of uniting the proletariat (working class) of all countries. I'm talking about all countries, not just China. You see, after all, my job is to issue orders to the proletariat, the workers, the comrades of the world.

S:

I will ask you again. Are you saying that, as a political system, you want to discard the CPC dictatorship system and really replace it with the Xi Empire?

XI'S G.S.:

Well, I mean, the parliamentary system will not last much longer. I don't think it has much more life in it. So, when the number of elder members diminishes, then I will give it some thought at that point.

I:

In this case, if you come to rule the world under the Xi Empire, what would you want to do? Do you have some sort of ideals?

XI'S G.S.:

Well, as a man, the basic impulse is the desire to rule as much as you can, right?

I:

So, it is basically your strong personal impulse?

XI'S G.S.:

Yes, of course that is the way I am. I mean, I already think the whole planet is mine. During my rule, I will end "the century of America."

Xi Jinping's guardian spirit: "democracy is deterioration"

A:

While I do think you are amazing, it is also said that within these six or seven years, there have been more than just 10 or 20 assassination attempts on your life.

XI'S G.S.:

Well, that is also something I enjoy.

A:

Ah, you enjoy it?

XI'S G.S.:

Well, you see, I get to implement a public execution when someone plans an assassination on me. When that happens, I can make an example out of that person and everyone snaps to attention. That is why having assassination attempts every now and then is fun for me. But of course, no one can ever escape from our control net, our information net.

A:

That said, you do not disclose where you are resting on a given day, and now...

XI'S G.S.:

I mean, I can disclose it, but...

S:

In that sense, changing your location and hiding your personage from sight is exactly what Qin Shi Huang did.

XI'S G.S.:

That is because I have a different level of power. Take Prime Minister Abe for example. All of his whereabouts are printed everywhere. The major mass media outlets all know where he is, all the time, you know? They release information that says things like, "Today, he jogged at a hotel," "He swam in a pool," or "He was in a sauna." It's a free kill. You could literally kill him anywhere, any time.

A:

That is exactly the reason why we are a civilized nation.

XI'S G.S.:

Look, there are tons of Chinese people working in, say, Roppongi for example. If we wanted to kill him, we could kill him at any time I wish. I do not even need a nuclear button. All I have to say is, "Will someone kill Abe tomorrow?" That would be the end of him.

S:

But you see, being transparent about the activities of politicians represents, in a sense, advancement in civilization and politics.

XI'S G.S.:

Why? That's not advancement, it's decline. What are you talking about? You all are already finished. Democracy is over. It's the end of the world of politics. OK? It's already dead.

And then, after that, the Xi Empire will start. The times will reset again and the Xi Kingdom will commence. That's what will bring about the world empire. You know, transportation has become very convenient now. The same is true of information. I mean, worldwide surveillance cameras will all be controlled by China. We will invite all the headquarters of American information- and internet-related companies to China. With that, we will be able to observe and record anything and everything all over the world in an instant. We will be able to know everything there is to know about where every single person is. What I am saying is, we will arrange things, so that we will be able to know even up to things like, "Right now, Abe entered the bathroom and he hasn't come out for ten minutes."

S:

I see. I guess for our part, we have to be careful about global internet corporations since they could be an easy link to China.

XI'S G.S.:

I mean, look, when the head editor of this little magazine of yours that only sells about a few tens of thousands of copies (*The Liberty*, a monthly magazine published by IRH Press Co., Ltd.) writes critical of Abe or the emperor, neither of them could even expunge you all. But if you all were to come into our country, there wouldn't be a tomorrow...

S:

That is democracy. It is the value of freedom.

XI'S G.S.:

You know, this democracy you speak of is flawed. It doesn't matter. What I am saying is that if you all came into China, there is no guarantee you would live to see the next day.

A:

I think the same thing is true for yourself as well.

XI'S G.S.:

What?

A:

Right now in China, what has become popular is wall newspapers, right?

XI'S G.S.:

What are you even talking about!? That's old. Very old.

A:

And they criticize you.

XI'S G.S.:

No, seriously, that's old.

Λ:

Well, but, in a sense, that is just a pointless cat-and-mouse, with security police also cracking down hard on the wall newspapers.

XI'S G.S.:

If that kind of thing were effective at all, you all could bring down your government with your fliers. Right?

A:

I mean, I do think that is a possibility, actually.

XI'S G.S.:

Heh, heh, heh, heh, heh [*laughs*]. No way. What are you talking about [*laughs*]?

A:

After all, even such primitive battles are one way to fight with words.

XI'S G.S.:

But you cannot even influence the miniscule police organization or security organization in Japan.

S:

All right, fair enough.

What could be Xi Jinping's blind spot?

S:

Our time is almost up, so I would like to focus on the core of today's discussion. First, I want to ask if there are currently any military blind spots for China somewhere near President Xi Jinping.

XI'S G.S.:

No.

S:

Do you have any blind spots in terms of economic problems?

XI'S G.S.:

No.

S:

Are there no blind spots in the political system as well?

XI'S G.S.:

No, there is none. And also, there are no blind spots in our space strategy.

S:

There are no blind spots, then.

XI'S G.S.:

I don't have any blind spots in terms of our information strategy, either. My plan for conquering Earth is progressing steadily. And in addition to that, we already have space technology that you all do not even know about yet.

S:

I would very much like to hear about that in more detail, but I want to set that aside for a separate occasion. Another thing I would like to ask today is, from the viewpoint of your plan for conquering

Earth, do you think the North Korea–United States Summit was a success?

XI'S G.S.:

Well, I mean, if you put it in *shogi* (Japanese chess) terms, it was basically a case of advancing a pawn and making them take it.

S:

Ah, I see.

XI'S G.S.:

It was a case of advancing a pawn, making them take it, and then suffering a loss. I mean, the feeling was one of placing a silver general from below the gold general. Something like that.

S:

I see. You are saying that you played that kind of a hand here. Also, are you going to take advantage of the North Korea–United States Summit or the U.S. and Japanese involvement in the Korean Peninsula to further strengthen the influential power of China?

XI'S G.S.:

Well, I think both the U.S. and Japan are currently headed for a hell of isolation, so you, underground church, should all think about how to survive.

A:

Currently, what we are seeing actually emerge in the Asian region is more of an anti-China trend.

XI'S G.S.:

There's no such kind of thing.

A:

If you want to talk about being isolated, I think that has more of a chance to come to pass for China instead.

XI'S G.S.:

Look, in about a decade, Japanese children will be learning Chinese instead of English from junior high school onward. Schools will be teaching Mandarin, you see. Because, if they do not, children will not be able to survive in the future.

S:

Today, you have spoken in extremely confident terms throughout the entire discussion. And we have also received all sorts of points to think about regarding how we should build our future. We want to communicate these words to people all over the world.

XI'S G.S.:

I thought it would be best to clarify a self-portrait of me for you, so that I can be better portrayed as a bad guy in the animation films you all make.* I am trying hard. I want you all to portray me very well in the enemy role. I am powerful enough to wash all of this away, you know?

S:

Right. I understand. For us as well, I feel that we have received highly important reference material for the Korean Peninsula problem as well as for the subsequent major issue, the China problem.

"To me, Trump is nothing more than a sheriff"

XI'S G.S.:

You all seem to be completely underestimating the level of my power and abilities, and you will wind up regretting that someday. And Trump? I mean, this guy is nothing more than a sheriff to me. I mean, from our viewpoint [*laughs*]. He doesn't even have any real power. He is nothing more than a sheriff.

---

* In the Happy Science animation movie *The Laws of the Universe −Part I* released October 2018 (executive producer and original story: Ryuho Okawa), there is an evil alien antagonist that tries to conquer Earth.

S:

The spirit of former United Kingdom Prime Minister Churchill has a completely different outlook on Trump, though.[†]

XI'S G.S.:

Oh, really? Hmm.

S:

I think that the fact that he only seems to have that level of power is actually a point that you would do well to be careful of.

XI'S G.S.:

If you are the reincarnation of Mao Zedong, I would listen to you, but we won't admit that.

The plan to control Japan through massive waves of Chinese immigrants

S:

[*To A and I.*] Are we done for today?

[†] Six days before this spiritual interview, Okawa recorded a spiritual interview with the spirit of former U.K. Prime Minister Winston Churchill. See *Beicho Kaidan go no Gaiko Senryaku Churchill no Reigen* (lit. "Diplomatic Strategy After the U.S.-North Korea Summit: Spiritual Interview with Churchill") (Tokyo: IRH Press, 2018).

XI'S G.S.:

Is that all? I mean, what exactly did I come here for today? This is it? Is this simple discussion good enough?

S:

Oh, no, really, you have spoken quite a bit...

A:

It is definitely enough.

XI'S G.S.:

All right then, you all just go ahead and try to sell your magazines in China, in Beijing. You'll be killed instantaneously. Hahaha [*laughs*].

A:

We believe that ultimately, the people of China want freedom, and they also want God.

XI'S G.S.:

They don't want that at all. The people of China just want food.

A:

I understand very well that you are not aware of the actual desires of your people.

XI'S G.S.:

No, all they want is food, and in addition to that, as long as they have money, they can go shopping abroad. The only thing in their heads is whether or not they can buy brand goods.

A:

If that were true, they would just be like simple animals.

XI'S G.S.:

Why do you say that? That is not true at all. I think that is just fine. For a human being, this is the biggest...

A:

I do not think that the people of China are like that.

S:

There is also a gradually increasing number of fans of Japan among the Chinese.

XI'S G.S.:

And the number of Japanese people is decreasing, though.

S:

Well, we do not know how that will pan out in the future yet.

XI'S G.S.:

Umm, there will be immigrants entering Japan very soon. Chinese immigrants will pour in, and they will control Japan for us. We also have a plan for controlling Japan. We have a plan to rule Japan through a massive wave of immigrants.

S:

I am aware of this. There's such kind of an idea.

"The North Korea–U.S. Summit was merely a puppet show by me"

S:

However, what matters is who has the stronger influential power.

XI'S G.S.:

And that is China, in the final analysis.

S:

We are grateful for having you speak your current thoughts and feelings today. Thank you very much for giving us this interview, six years since the last time we spoke.

XI'S G.S.:

I am basically overflowing with surplus energy. I mean, even this North Korea–U.S. Summit event was merely a puppet show by me. That is how I see it. [*To A.*] Too bad, *Sankei Shimbun**. So long, Sankei Shimbun. Good bye! Ahahaha [*laughs*].

S:

Our publication is the monthly magazine, *The Liberty* [*laughs*].

XI'S G.S.:

Ah, was that it? It wasn't the Sankei? Ah, I didn't know that.

S:

Thank you for your precious words today. Thank you very much.

---

*A is a former journalist for Sankei Shimbun.

Chapter FIVE

Spiritual Interview with the Guardian Spirit of Vladimir Putin (Excerpt)

Recorded on November 9, 2018
at Special Lecture Hall, Happy Science
Tokyo, Japan

1

How to Work with Trump in Fluctuating Times

Why is Russiagate flaming?

A:

I would like to ask a bit about the U.S. Recently, the midterm elections were held, and unfortunately the ruling Republican Party did not win majority in the House. This resulted in a slight disadvantage for Trump in terms of power. And, within this backdrop, there is Russiagate that has resulted in constant investigation over two long years already. While ultimately nothing has come of those investigations, they will be pursuing him even more in the legislature. Would you like to comment on the Russiagate matter?

VLADIMIR PUTIN'S GUARDIAN SPIRIT:

Since the U.S. is a nation of immigrants and there are many races there, so are there a lot of lobbyists and people with different interests. And if you want to talk about that, while the Jews do not have the numbers, they do have much power. They own media resources and have financial power as well. For example, they made Jerusalem the capital (of Israel). In terms of democracy, the

Jewish people have a disproportionate amount of power. So, that is one thing.

In addition to that, there are also a lot of lobbyists for China and, basically, spies working for the nation—students and researchers who put a lot of thought into studying or placing themselves in companies temporarily as researchers to steal American software and take it back home. So, right now the U.S. is being subject to an amazing amount of theft. And so, they are doing these kinds of things just enough to stay under the radar. Russia was targeted simply because it was easier to fuel the antipathy of the American people. That is why they are told, "President Trump is being friends with Russia and alienating places like Mexico and Canada."

A:

It seems that the U.S., including the FBI and the CIA, just can't change the mindset it had toward the Soviet Union during the Cold War.

PUTIN'S G.S.:

Yes, yes, yes.

A:

The truth is that the U.S. also has to work together with Russia if it wants to continue onward, but they just keep moving in the negative direction out of habit.

PUTIN'S G.S.:

I mean, we have this agreement to reduce nuclear weapons that Obama and I talked about so much and decided on, but now, President Trump has started to say they're going to scrap this. Of course, I understand that Russia is not the only target of this, though. This is also intended as a threat toward China and North Korea, as I see it. So, I think if the U.S. had continued to go in an Obama-like direction, right now negotiations with North Korea would probably have turned out even worse. It will only be a matter of time before China treats the U.S. as an easy opponent. Because if China surpassed the U.S. economically, they would definitely subsequently make a move to become a nuclear superpower. Thus, if the U.S. were to keep up with nuclear reduction, the balance of power would gradually start to flip. Power would flip both economically and militarily. And if that happened, the U.S. would be in a position where it would have to kowtow to the desires of China.

And if you ask what the U.S. needs to do to avoid that, well obviously what they should really do is improve relations with Russia and let Japan have a little more power as well. They simply have to be able to make those kinds of strategic judgments.

What happened in the 2-hour one-on-one talk at the U.S.–Russia Summit in Helsinki?

A:

Talking about the U.S.-Russia relations, I think we can see some progress in this with President Trump specifically aiming to work as a team with Russia. At the outset of the U.S.–Russia Summit in Helsinki this past July (2018), President Trump and President Putin talked alone for two hours. Most of what was discussed is still unknown, but according to what was leaked afterward, Dr. Kissinger said something along the lines of, "This was a conference that very much needed to happen right away. It was very good that it happened."

Based on these things, some are speculating that the two probably worked out some kind of strategy to oppose China. Could you tell us what really happened?

PUTIN'S G.S.:

Well, "opposing China" has not proceeded sufficiently yet. Trump's position is that he has to completely defeat North Korea, but there is always the possibility that North Korea will escape like a slippery eel. North Korea could definitely get away if China takes on a different attitude. Trump wants to clear up at the least the North Korea problem in his first four years of presidency. So, if only Russia would clearly state they will not help prolong North's existence... You know, as things stand now, the two paths North Korea has for survival are insurance from either Russia or China, or from both. Or another option is for them to unify the Koreas peacefully, but actually take the initiative. I mean it would be a long and difficult matter about who takes the initiative, the one with the money or the one with nuclear weapons.

These three approaches are basically the only stratagems

available to them, so they definitely need some very clever strategy and tactics.

A:

I see. So, at the U.S.–Russia Summit, the North Korean problem was the main topic discussed?

PUTIN'S G.S.:

Well, I mean, currently, Trump views China neutrally. He feels there is room to think about further relations with them if the U.S. shakes them up and that causes them to fall in line. But if they do not fall in line, then his thinking is basically, "Now is the time to teach them about how frightening the U.S. can be, otherwise they would eventually stop falling in line."

O:

I believe that in the joint press-conference with both men after the talks, they mainly talked about Syria. However, within secret talks between just the two men, I imagine that all sorts of other things were discussed. For example, did you talk about the Ukrainian problem?

PUTIN'S G.S.:

Well, look, Trump is surprisingly understanding. He knows why Russia would want to go to war to protect Ukraine. The American media cannot understand it. Europe cannot understand, either. Trump understands. He would do the exact same thing. If he were the president of Russia, he would definitely do the same thing, no questions asked. And that is why he totally gets it. He understands. However, the mass media cannot understand.

O:

But of course, President Trump has not yet said anything publicly regarding that.

PUTIN'S G.S.:

Well, of course he cannot say anything. But he understands. Because he himself would do the same. I completely think he would do the same.

O:

What we can see is that the economic sanctions on Russia over the Ukrainian situation since the Obama administration are still in place, though. So, does President Trump want to lift these at some point?

PUTIN'S G.S.:

Well, you see, he is operating in response to what is happening with the EU. And it seems like the U.S. is trying to stir things up with Europe as well, you see. They are inspiring British independence and even French independence. The truth is, he is trying to create something different, right? I can totally understand his way of thinking on this. He is lining up the true economic powers around the world in order of strength and trying to team up with the top countries only. That is what he is really doing. He generally feels that conglomerations that have a lot of weak hangers-on, like the EU, are basically meaningless. You know, he thinks that, for example, teaming up with places like Mexico would only end up with Mexico just taking from the U.S. He thinks so, unlike those groups.

Weak point of democracy— poor administrative efficiency

PUTIN'S G.S.:

I do not know how far Trump can dive into the Chinese problem, because he has always the problem of presidential terms. And I mean, we saw this in the results of the midterm election as well, but basically there is a risk of the Democratic Party getting back in power in the next U.S. presidential election. So, he has to produce some sort of results in his first term. In the U.S., elections take up a lot of energy, you know? It's a heavy matter, and the mass media mounts all sorts of attacks with lots of scandals and the like, right? In Russia it is very easy to silence that sort of thing.

A:

Well, yes.

PUTIN'S G.S.:

It really is easy. All you have to say is, "You won't get home," and it will be over. You just have to say things like, "I hope you get home safely."

A:

Some journalists were already targeted.

PUTIN'S G.S.:

Or, if you just say one simple thing like, "Your daughter goes to XYZ School, right? Classes are dismissed at three o'clock." If you just have this kind of a chat in a hallway or something like that, everyone basically just shuts up. They already know exactly what that means, so that's enough.

R:

So, you have no intention of changing that basic nature of yours?

PUTIN'S G.S.:

Well, I do not mean it in that way. I am only talking about administrative efficiency. I am not trying to say that I am some sort of evil leader. The administrative efficiency is the issue. Democracy is all fine and well, but you can definitely say that its administrative efficiency is too low.

2

How to Contain China

What is Putin's opinion on Vice President Pence's historic address on October 4?

A:

Regarding U.S.-China relations, one major move in the last couple months has been Vice President Pence's address on October 4, 2018 which largely overturned the policy toward China. In this speech, he brought up all of the points involved including trade, human rights suppression, and religious suppression. The U.S. has already been thinking about these things, but this time he clearly said that they have no choice but to oppose China. What do you think of this?

PUTIN'S G.S.:

For now, the U.S. is demonstrating their dissatisfaction for China regarding North Korea. If China strengthens its pipe to North Korea again and secretly plans to prolong their existence, and keeps trying to use them as a wall for a long time, then we cannot rely on China to help resolve the North Korean problem. That's one concern. Basically, from China's perspective, preserving the lips (North Korea) will protect the teeth (China). So, Pence's strategy is to use that against them. That's what I think.

So, ultimately, what comes after "America First" is America's self-awareness as the world's policeman, as number one and as the one to lead the world this century. Although they may seem egocentric, it is also true that they are protecting the order of the world as the number one country. So, I mean, your... what should I call it? Your "Spiritual Interview with the Guardian Spirit of Merkel"*?

A:

Right.

PUTIN'S G.S.:

OK. In it, the guardian spirit of Chancellor Merkel said something along the lines of, "Both the U.S. and China think that their domestic laws are international law." I mean, since Merkel is saying this as the person who has gathered some twenty or so of the smallest and weakest nations in the EU, I guess that actually is the case. I think that the U.S. making its own domestic law the international law was a good thing in the sense that they took leadership after WWII. We do need to put the brakes on that a bit, though.

However, think about the domestic law of China becoming international law. The actual laws that would apply are a bit frightening. Earlier, I spoke of improving administrative efficiency, but in the case of China, their administrative efficiency is too high. It's just too high. It is so overly high that there is no room for opposition parties [*laughs*]. I mean, even we have some. We have opposition parties in Russia.

---

*See Chapter 6.

A:

Yes, it is a democracy.

PUTIN'S G.S.:

We have freedom of religion and also freedom of speech. We are not as strict as China, you see. We are quite a bit more democratic than that.

China's intelligence level has not improved since the time of Emperor Qin Shi Huang

R:

I would very much like to hear your frank feelings about China. What are your thoughts about Xi Jinping? For example, when Master Ryuho Okawa recorded a spiritual interview with the guardian spirit of Xi Jinping in June this year, he said things like, "Russia should also be split into three"...

PUTIN'S G.S.:

Hahaha [*laughs*]. Really!?

R:

... "They have fallen to the number nine country in the world," and "They can never be a significant world power." So, apparently this is the way Xi Jinping honestly thinks of Russia.

PUTIN'S G.S.:

Really? Well, if he is saying those kinds of insolent things, you all must launch a counterattack. There was a time when China was only one-tenth of Japan. They might have come this far, but they have no right to be telling you that, so you should definitely mount a counterattack. Japan striking back economically would really be good for world peace. China does not need to be anything more than a semi-developed country. With the way they do things, they should never ever be a developed country. The country has not learned at all from 2,500 years ago... or maybe 2,000 years ago. In any case, what I mean to say is that there has been no change in their level since Qin Shi Huang, the first emperor of the Qin Dynasty. If such a country becomes the world leader, that would be horrible.

So, Islam and China, if the world were to be completely covered by these two, that would be like having the entire globe be hijacked by the currently popular Venom (from the movie, *Venom* [Sony Pictures Releasing, 2018]). You know? That is what it would be like. It would be Hell.

A:

Recently (September 11 – 17), Russia and China held the largest military exercise since the Cold War, and people think that this is certainly dangerous.

PUTIN'S G.S.:

Umm, we are not doing that because we want to, you know? I do not actually want to be doing that, but internationally, I have to show the world that we can team up with anyone, in any way. The message is, "If you do not want us to do this, lift the economic sanctions on Russia." Also, I want to tell everyone to return to the original G8. Regarding this, one problem is that Merkel is too stubborn and another is that the American fake news media are too ignorant. They just do not see their real national interest and the correct way of looking at the world.

R:

So, do you mean Vostok 2018 (name of the military exercise) was a warning? Was it a way of saying, "If you push us too far, Russia could very likely team up even with China"?

PUTIN'S G.S.:

Exactly. If you would sign a peace treaty with us, we would not mind doing military exercises with Japan instead.

Why a Japan-Russia peace treaty must be signed soon

O:

In terms of China's military strength, this might work opposite to the joint exercises, but currently, China's naval strength is increasing tremendously and they seem to be going after the Arctic Ocean sea lane. If this happens, will they be a threat to Russia as well?

PUTIN'S G.S.:

Ah, yes, the Arctic Ocean sea lane. Well, that might be a bit difficult. China is looking farther and farther south, and the Arctic Ocean isn't very... there are no food provisions, you know? So, that is less likely. If they are going to do something like that, their only purpose would be to take the area near the U.K. that has offshore oil, or perhaps it would be quicker to take the Middle East.

R:

The idea of the Arctic Ocean sea lane is a topic of focus along with the One Belt, One Road Initiative. The general opinion is that success in both of these areas will make securing resources, including oil, easy.

PUTIN'S G.S.:

Are you saying there is oil in Russia as well?

R:

There seem to be petroleum and gas hidden in the Arctic Ocean, and there has even been news coverage saying that China is aiming for this. They think that traveling the Arctic Ocean sea lane saves more time rather than taking the traditional route from China through the South China Sea and the Suez Canal to get around to the Middle East and Europe.

PUTIN'S G.S.:

Well, there are a lot of nations out there, so there is always the chance of having some sort of trouble mid-route from some country. That is definitely part of it. But you know, it seems like they have become aware that Ryuho Okawa is going to places like India and Sri Lanka* and trying to block China's One Belt, One Road Initiative.

A:

That is true. The administration flipped and went from pro-China to anti-China.

PUTIN'S G.S.:

Right. The Philippines and Malaysia, and basically everyone stops being pro-China after he visits. And the same is true of Taiwan. I imagine that, from China's perspective, there are still a lot of enemies in this area, so they want to think of a different route. But Russia is not that easy of a pushover either, you know? Note that, if the EU and the U.S. make some sort of pincer attack on us and if even Japan joins in that, and they all use that as a strategy to try to isolate Russia, then we will have to give a bit more thought. That is exactly why I am currently saying to hurry and sign (a Japan-Russia peace treaty). When a president clarifies the national strategy approach, it cannot be changed so easily. Thus, I am saying to hurry up and give us a response exactly because of this.

I am a spirit, a guardian spirit, but I used to live as a Japanese†, so

---

*The author has given a total of nine lectures in English, in his missionary tour across Asia in 2011: India and Nepal in March, the Philippines and Hong Kong in May, Singapore and Malaysia in September, and Sri Lanka in November.

I can actually read Japanese. After Ryuho Okawa's younger daughter returned to Japan from Moscow State University, I heard that she reported to him. But you know, actually, we also kept watch over her. Anyhow, she reported to him that economic sanctions on Russia are not working. Right now, that is true. They are not working much at all. I mean, yes, it is also true that we are working hard to make it look like they are not working as much as possible. And apparently, she even waited two hours to watch me (President Putin) come out of the Kremlin. If only the Russian embassy had noticed just a bit sooner, we could have at least offered her a cup of tea or something inside the Kremlin. Hmm, the embassy did not do enough behind the scenes. But also, the Happy Science temple needs to get a bit larger. A bit larger, you know? In any case, right now, I am giving my opinion behind the scenes, so that you do not get treated like Aum Shinrikyo.

A:

Thank you very much.

PUTIN'S G.S.:

I am saying things like we must not treat you in that way, but you know… We received a bit of damage from Aum Shinrikyo[‡], and

---

[†] According to spiritual research conducted by Happy Science, Putin was likely born as Emperor Shomu who built the Great Buddha statue in 8th century Japan, and as the 8th Tokugawa shogun, Yoshimune.

[‡] Aum Shinrikyo built a branch in Moscow and acquired members there in the 1990s. The religious group was the source of many social problems in Japan, such as the Tokyo subway sarin gas attack in 1995. In 2001, its Russian followers were arrested in Japan for attempted terrorism, and in 2016, Russia declared it as a terrorist group and banned its activities.

there are still remnants of that, you know? There are still remnants of Aum Shinrikyo, so it is still a bit difficult for people to see the difference between them and you. People are still a bit cautious. You need to hurry up and do a lecture session in Russia. Hurry up and come to Russia.

3

Putin's Faith, Thoughts, and Creed

At the ceremony, Putin made the sign of the cross as he watched the video of an atomic bomb

O:

Ever since you became president, freedom of religion in Russia really has been expanding quite a bit.

PUTIN'S G.S.:

I accept it. I have accepted it. Yes, yes.

O:

And this is not only true for the Russian Orthodox Church, but for Islam and other religions as well. Are we to understand that you have some sort of...

PUTIN'S G.S.:

Look, I do have faith. I have it, and I also understand the need for freedom of religion. Thus, I can understand how Ukraine wants to split off from the Russian Orthodox Church and establish their own Ukrainian Orthodox Church. I have not gone as far as Xi Jinping who represses religion and thinks everyone who believes in religion is crazy, you know? Because, you see, I do fully believe in God.

R:

During the 70th anniversary ceremony of the Invasion of Normandy (June 6, 2014), President Putin was among the people who went to France. In the performances put on at that time, there was a video of the mushroom cloud that formed when the atomic bomb was dropped on Hiroshima. When that image came up on the screen, the audience applauded and then-President Obama clapped as he chewed gum. In contrast, you immediately made the sign of the cross. This just happened to be captured on camera by a news coverage...

PUTIN'S G.S.:

Oh? What news company?

R:

I believe it must have been TBS.

PUTIN'S G.S.:

Is that a Japanese television station?

R:

Yes, it is Japanese. You can still see that video on the internet today...

PUTIN'S G.S.:

Ah. Yes. Well, that certainly is a good shot, a good angle.

R:

Yes, I too was extremely impressed. I felt that you showed us that your faith is genuine, and showed us your human side, which is to say, a side of you that is different from leaders of materialistic countries. Regarding the future conception of Russia, are you willing to continue working to create a new Russia with faith as its pillar?

PUTIN'S G.S.:

Hmm. There is the idea that Japan will experience a recession due to economy, namely trade with China, and South Korea is speaking nonsense such as, "You must pay restitution salaries for wartime laborers from over 70 years ago." I think that kind of country should just sink into the ocean. They have a beggar-like nature. It is unpleasant. I do not like those kinds of people who approach you with dirty, lice-infested clothes and say, "Give me money." That is an old way of thinking. They are behind. They are clearly behind the times. That is the South Korean populism, right? I mean, it's just shameful...

"I advocate faith, freedom, and democracy, and make decisions by myself"

R:

I would very much like to hear your political philosophy. That would be a magnificent lesson for us.

PUTIN'S G.S.:

Oh! Sure, come at me.

R:

The Happiness Realization Party wishes to create a new world order under the keyword, faith. I would be honored if you could tell us how you see the world, what direction you want to take Russia in, and what the core of your ideas on these issues are.

PUTIN'S G.S.:

Well, you all keep saying, "freedom, democracy, and faith," right? I am different. Faith [*pounds desk once*] should come first. Faith is the most important [*pounds table twice*]. I would even go so far as to arrange in the order, "faith, freedom, and democracy." For me, this is the correct order. So, faith is important. Creating a country of God is a very important thing. And I think Trump agrees with me on this, probably. He also has faith, too. He believes in God...

O:

We heard this in your last spiritual interview, too. You said something like, "freedom only comes when there is faith."

PUTIN'S G.S.:

Well, if I did, then that is proof that we are the same person. Look, I said all sorts of things, but when I talk to the Japanese prime minister, sadly the discussion is not like that. The discussion always just seems trifling and small. He is someone who is not mentally flexible, and he would be much better off talking about in a more substantive way. How can I put it? I mean, I imagine that he is coming from the approach of a framework built by government officials. He is probably in a situation where, unless he gets approval from the bureaucrats, he cannot simply speak his mind. But we are a bit different in that respect. Sure, we need bureaucrats to get information, but it is the top leader who makes decisions and takes action.

I think Trump is exactly the same in this regard. Well, yes, he gathers information through bureaucrats, but he does what he wants to do on his own, right? Twitter is actually a form of media that has the best quality in the world, right? I mean, for him.

A:

Right, that is true. Yes. Let us go back to the earlier discussion of creating a country of God. It may sound rude, but I've read that the Russian Orthodox Church is slightly different from other Christian groups in that it apparently embraces the idea of a unity with God. I have read that the idea of becoming one with God is a solid part of this tradition. I am under the impression that you are attempting to build a country where people grow toward God with this idea as the pillar. Would this be correct?

PUTIN'S G.S.:

Hmm. Well, if you put it like that, it gets difficult to tell me apart from Xi Jinping, so it's hard to say. You know, to accept the existence of God does not link directly to making all people equal in the communist sense, but there is an aspect of admonishing the arrogance of those in power. So, while I myself am a person in power, I must never be arrogant. God exists for that purpose. Because, you see, a human being should never be regarded as the ultimate leader. I mean, having a human be a leader through election only is not necessarily a good thing. That person is merely a leader on behalf of God, and if he goes against God's will, then he should be fired. If democracy can function in that way, then it is functioning properly. But if, instead, it is merely made up from things like the majority in this world, the amount of distributed money, or combined power of fake news, then that is not quite right. Something completely opposite of that can form. The existence of God and religion is needed in order to make sure something completely opposite does not generate a majority.

According to your spiritual readings, hadn't Jesus Christ or people close to that level been born as Russian literary giants*? I know all of this, you see. I have all the basic information. It has been passed up to me. I mean, I do have a division that is in charge of investigating you.

A:

Ah, is that so?

PUTIN'S G.S.:

I basically know all of your past declarations, basic ways of thinking about things. And I'm considering how they should turn out in the future. If you don't mind Russia being involved just a bit more in this, I can do things for you, but I am trying to stay behind the scenes because I feel that it is better to make it look as if you are achieving success under your own free efforts.

---

*According to spiritual research conducted by Happy Science, Tolstoy and Dostoevsky are both a part of a savior's soul: Tolstoy is a part of Jesus Christ, and Dostoevsky is a part of Zoroaster (Zarathustra).

O:

I see.

Putin understands financial reform and the generation of wealth

O:

You just spoke about the ethical side of religion. I think that it is definitely true that when the USSR crumbled and Russia all of a sudden became a free nation, it did not immediately become a capitalist country in the true sense. Before Putin became president, mafia or fraudulent groups were powerful in Russia. However, it seems when he rebuilt Russia, he was trying to show the people some kind of ethical framework and the true spirit of capitalism through Christianity, the Russian Orthodox Church. Is this accurate?

PUTIN'S G.S.:

Yes. That is true. So, I understand things like financial reform and generating wealth because my soul experienced those things. Unlike Muslim people, I do understand things like the wonderfulness of the great statues of Buddha. To Muslims, these might just be objects to be destroyed, but I understand. Of course, there are different Christian churches in different places around the world, so I do not think this is the universal Christian opinion. Anyway, how can I say this? I do understand. I understand what it means to have faith in something great and wanting to put that into physical form. And I understand it is better for politics and the economy to run smoothly based on that.

And you know, I have said this before, so it might sound like empty flattery, but even though the Japanese mass media and the like might not place much importance on this, the only Japanese person I trust is Mr. Ryuho Okawa. In other words, I feel that there is no one else who takes responsibility for their own words. Lots of different weird, small movements pop up and disappear soon after, getting in your way. To us, it seems like they are doing that to you (the Happiness Realization Party), preventing you from making a presence. But I am praying that you pave a straight road into the core of Japanese culture.

4

The Reason Putin Was Born in This Age

Straighten out your thoughts about China

R:

Excuse me. At the Eastern Economic Forum (held September 12, 2018), Prime Minister Abe said in front of President Putin something like, "If not now, when? If we do not do it, who else will?" He proposed a new relationship with Russia as if to say, "Now is the time!" I imagine that President Putin took this positively since he said so. We too would definitely like to do whatever we could to make it possible to quickly sign a Japan-Russia peace treaty...

PUTIN'S G.S.:

Please do what you can. And even regarding the Uyghurs, if you want to do something, you need to involve Russia. It would be horrible for China to get done in from behind. This would be hard on them. The way Russia would work will be a pain for China. Also, he (Okawa) sent a message to Germany[*], right? The message was to change the way they think. The idea was, "Look, Kant[†], this whole idea of prioritizing trade with China first and foremost to make money is quite a problem." "You need a more just cause." "Are you really OK with turning a blind eye to a place that is so involved in suppressing human rights and buying and selling human organs? You shouldn't allow them to make money like that." They have to straighten out their thoughts about these things.

And there is another reason I want to sign a Japan-Russia peace treaty this year (2018). General Heihachiro Togo[‡] was reborn in Japan. We Russians also respect him.

---

[*] See Chapter 1.

[†] According to spiritual research conducted by Happy Science, German Chancellor Merkel was likely born as Immanuel Kant in her past life. See Chapter 6.

[‡] Heihachiro Togo (1848–1934) was an admiral of the Imperial Japanese Navy. He was considered a hero, to the people of Japan and the world, for defeating Russia in the Russo-Japanese War.

A:

Oh?

R:

So, there is a big spiritual meaning...

PUTIN'S G.S.:

Heihachiro Togo was reborn in Japan. This is very significant! To a great extent. Yes. If you are going to fight, then please, I want you to fight China. I want you to fight China, not Russia.

A:

I see [*laughs*]. Russia was defeated by Heihachiro Togo (in the Battle of Tsushima in the Russo-Japanese War), after all.

PUTIN'S G.S.:

Please, leave Russia out of your fights. I'm begging you. We have had enough. We do not want another round of it. We do not want another "perfect game." Please do that with China instead. I felt we need to sign a peace treaty as soon as possible when I heard that Heihachiro Togo was reborn.

A:

Ah, I see.

PUTIN'S G.S.:

In the spiritual sense, the movement is picking up speed. The situation is dangerous. Japan is already preparing itself for another round, so we are in danger.

R:

So, your proposal is to work together with us to contain China?

PUTIN'S G.S.:

Hmm, I mean, China would be a good choice, right? I mean, China is an evil country. Right? Letting an evil country get rich is not a good thing, right? They should not be allowed to get that rich. So, you should build up your economy a bit more by working with others and use that money for further growth. China, which suppresses human rights and is a "problem country" as a permanent member of the UN council, is showing its power and trying to make a world of two superpowers, China and the U.S. That must be crushed.

If Japan... I mean, Russia does not necessarily have to surpass Japan economically, though. We do not mind being in third place. We do not have to be in second place. Third is just fine, but I do not want to see the day Japan loses to Mexico or Indonesia. Also, the word is that you will be surpassed by India as well. They are saying that the Japanese economy is going to be surpassed by countries like India, Mexico, and Indonesia. This is too sad. I want Japan to be more of a hero.

Putin was chosen as the person to rebuild the post-USSR Russia

A:

So, do you mean that the major factor played in you being born in Russia was the relationship with Japan?

PUTIN'S G.S.:

Well, I mean, modernization of Russia is also very important. The Russian problem, which is to say the USSR problem, was basically the biggest threat after WWII. And we knew how much time would pass until the USSR crumbles, about how many years it would take until it crumbles, so there was a plan in the heavenly world how it should be rebuilt after that. This is why I was chosen and why I'm here now. It's like, I want to improve Japan-Russia relations during my time. And Abe? Abe was probably Tokiyori Hojo* or someone like that in his past life, right? And he was, umm, you know, preparing to fight with the China-Korea (Yuan-Goryeo) coalition force, right? The same sort of thing is happening now.

---

* Tokiyori Hojo was a regent of the Kamakura shogunate in 13th century Japan. According to spiritual research conducted by Happy Science, Japanese Prime Minister Abe was likely born as Hojo in his past life.

A:

I see. You were "sent down from the heavenly world," so who do you generally receive guidance from?

PUTIN'S G.S.:

Well, I am generally a Christian, so I am receiving the power of Christ. But at the same time, the land of Russia is culturally connected all the way to Northern Europe and has a mutual relationship that goes even as far as Germany, in truth. I have Christ as the central axis right now, so my feeling is that we can be Westernized. However, on a deeper level, we have the god Odin[†]. Odin does not show up much to you guys, right? He watches over the area from Northern Europe to Russia. Yes.

A:

Ah, is that so?

PUTIN'S G.S.:

Yes, Odin currently watches mainly over the colder countries over here.

A:

I see.

[†] Odin is the chief god of Norse mythology. According to spiritual research conducted by Happy Science, he was an actual king of Asgard who lived sometime around 8,000 to 9,000 years ago. He established Asgard, a civilization centered around Northern Europe. Odin is one of the branch spirits of El Cantare, God of the Earth.

R:

I believe you have an extremely deep connection to Shakyamuni, to Buddha.

PUTIN'S G.S.:

That is true.

R:

In that sense, President Putin was selected by the heavenly world to create the next world order. Was that the plan?

PUTIN'S G.S.:

So, right now what is expected is... I mean, Trump and myself as well are being referred to as dictators by everyone, as is Merkel, but the truth is that the heavenly world is sending powerful people in an attempt to somehow reform the world. I want to make some progress during our time. I want to do whatever I can. I feel that even though we are in different countries, we can work under a universal set of values. So, unless Japanese politicians become a bit more religious, we cannot be on the same page.

A:

Speaking of dictators, Turkey and Saudi Arabia are countries of concern. The Turkish president and the Saudi Arabian crown prince, we can't clearly label them as dictators, though.

PUTIN'S G.S.:

Well, the thing is, this is small. As a problem, it is small, perhaps. It might be a secondary concern or maybe less than a tertiary concern. Much larger problems would definitely be... a potential worldwide war between the Islamic world and Israel with its supporting countries such as the U.S. and the U.K. So, the Islamic world has to be changed a bit as well. We (the Russian Federation) have Islamic republics within us as well. Of course, in our case Christianity is the state religion, though. We had Muslim countries in the old USSR as well, and to put it bluntly, this is a difficult thing. In short, you end up with two separate sovereignties.

A:

One country close to Russia is, of course, Syria. And Iran is also relatively close. It is extremely difficult to control these two countries. What are your current thoughts on this?

PUTIN'S G.S.:

There is a lot of religious struggle there. And Iran is a developed nation in religious terms. So, these people have sense of values that they just will not compromise. Iran claims to be the holy land of an older religion, older than Christianity and Judaism, so they will not give it up easily. Everyone knows that Israel has nuclear arms. This is backed by the U.S. behind the scenes, although they haven't officially said so, right?

A:

Right.

PUTIN'S G.S.:

The logic is that it is fine for Israel to have nuclear weapons, in other words a Jewish country that should in theory have been against Christianity, but not fine for any Islamic country to have nuclear weapons. Well, of course, Pakistan does have nuclear arms, though. This logic that no other Islamic countries besides Pakistan can have nuclear weapons is another source of concern. I cannot help but feel that this really is another example of racial prejudice.

Some even say that Israel's military power is probably about fourth in the world, or even that they might actually be the second most powerful. They have such advanced nuclear weapons. Their power of the air force could put them on an almost level playing field with the air force of America, which is the most advanced in the world. The U.S. is taken over by Jewish capital, so basically, they just keep selling various technologies including flight technology to Israel. They are immensely slow on selling to Japan. And even though technology seems to have finally started percolating in since Trump took charge, it is still true that technology was already integrated into Israel first. Thus, if they were to fight Arabic fighter jets with their air force, the Arab forces would be entirely shot down without the loss of a single Israeli jet. That is the difference in fighting strength, you see. But it is still unclear whether a deal can be reached on this.

American evangelical Christians were calling to recover Jerusalem. Thus, Trump actualized one wish from the people that have supported him, but there is still a major problem in this scenario, and he still has yet to set about solving it. However, um, Iran... Iran is also kind of pro-Japanese in some ways. It is a pro-Japanese country, so there is room for Japan to participate a bit more. Because it is pro-Japanese. Also, to Christian countries, Syria is a significant place because Jesus walked there. And the disciples of Jesus did as well. So, I want this area to be a bit more peaceful, but it does seem that there is a possibility it will become the next flashpoint. So, concerning the area from Syria to around Turkey, first of all we have to bring an end to war there and make it a peaceful region. We just do not know the true origins of these guerillas in the area. We have to somehow prevent the general public from getting massacred. Military strength is generally thought of as evil by the mass media, but in order to protect your country from being trampled by mere guerilla forces, I think it is better to have some kind of military strength in the long run.

A:
I am a bit curious about Russian military strength. It is often said that you probably have aliens in your military...

PUTIN'S G.S.:
Hahahahaha [*laughs*].

A:

And I mean, the U.S. has them also, and it is said that China does as well. Regarding this, could you enlighten us, especially the Japanese people?

PUTIN'S G.S.:

Well, as far as our ability to explore outer space, we beat the U.S. to that. When they made atomic bombs we made hydrogen bombs. Then, we went out into space. There was some competition between us, but now, we do not have that much economic power. We do have the technology, though, of course. However, I do think it is very strange for Japan of all places to be behind Russia. You should be just as far along as us, really. And as far as space goes, well, what is going on with aliens is classified information, you know? It is confidential. It is just not something a president can go on talking about to another country. And especially with my past in an intelligence agency, this is something I have to be careful about. A loose mouth could cost me my life.

R:

When we summoned the guardian spirit of Mr. Xi Jinping recently, he went so far as to say, "As a permanent member of the UN council, alien technology licensing is standard practice." So, should we understand that the U.K. and France are also involved in this?

PUTIN'S G.S.:

Yes. They have landed in France. Yes. The U.K. also knows about this, as does the U.S. The U.S. has brought in this tech on a massive scale. And Russia has already gone so far as to take in a lot of help into the military, from aliens to supernaturally gifted people. We do not deny spiritual things. We hire a lot of supernaturally gifted people, even in the military. I mean, just having someone like Mr. Ryuho Okawa alone would give us the power of ten divisions.

R:

Well, I think that would be quite more than just ten divisions...

PUTIN'S G.S.:

Ah, yes, it could be even more powerful, yes.

R:

Do you yourself have some sort of alien roots...

PUTIN'S G.S.:

Alien? Umm, well, I probably should not talk about that sort of thing very much. The Japanese media would not believe me even if I did.

R:

Ah, yes, that is true. I apologize.

Spiritual Interview with the Guardian Spirit of Angela Merkel (Excerpt)

Recorded on September 28, 2018
at Special Lecture Hall, Happy Science
Tokyo, Japan

1
"My Aim is to Make One Organization for World Peace"

ANGELA MERKEL'S GUARDIAN SPIRIT:

Uh. *Guten Morgen* ("Good morning" in German).

M:

Guten Morgen. Are you the guardian spirit of Chancellor Merkel?

MERKEL'S G.S.:

Yeah.

M:

Thank you very much for coming to Happy Science today. We are so happy to have you here. I'm so excited to have a talk with you. Thank you very much.

MERKEL'S G.S.:

Be cool. Behave yourself.

M:

OK. Behave myself. OK. You became the first female chancellor in 2005. Since then, you have led Germany, the most powerful country of the EU, for these 13 years.

MERKEL'S G.S.:

Thank you, thank you, thank you very much.

M:

I respect you so much. And you are well known as the most powerful lady in the world, so my first...

MERKEL'S G.S.:

What is the meaning of "lady"?

M:

Lady? No, no, I just... [*Laughs.*]

A:

Are you saying that you seem like a man... [*Laughs.*]

MERKEL'S G.S.:

Most powerful "person."

M:

Person. I'm sorry. I made a mistake. So, you are the most powerful "leader" in the world.

MERKEL'S G.S.:

OK. Better.

M:

OK. Thank you. So, my first question is, "What is the source of your leadership?"

MERKEL'S G.S.:

Denken ("Think" in German). Ah. Think. Continue thinking. And make good decisions. That's all.

M:

So, when you make decisions, what are the criteria or thinking you have?

MERKEL'S G.S.:

Firstly, study harder and harder. Next, listen to the opinions of famous people and then listen to the common people. And lastly, please listen to the voice of God and think within you. Obey your conscience and make a decision. OK?

M:

Yes, Thank you very much.

A:

You said to listen to the voice of God. Could you tell us your viewpoint of faith?

MERKEL'S G.S.:

Viewpoint of faith? Formally, I'm a Christian. Formally. Traditional Christian in Germany.

M:

But...

MERKEL'S G.S.:

"But"? But? No, it's a conclusion, so no.

C:

What kind of faith do you have right now?

MERKEL'S G.S.:

I have faith in God. Large print God.

M:

G-O-D?

MERKEL'S G.S.:

Oh, yeah.

M:

So, you believe in the Creator?

MERKEL'S G.S.:

Yeah, not only Jesus Christ, but God. Printed in large "G".

C:

Does it mean El Cantare?

MERKEL'S G.S.:

You call him so, but it must be the conclusion, so never ask me too much.

A:

Your approval rating is falling now. Your political power is getting weaker now.

MERKEL'S G.S.:

Getting weaker... Oh, you're insulting me?

A:

No, no, no, no. This situation is very severe for you. How do you see your political situation?

MERKEL'S G.S.:

It's OK. I'm old enough. I'm 64. Now is the time I must leave this dirty world. I'll do my best to the end of my chancellor period, but

I don't like this kind of dirty and too much emotional world of politics.* I studied a logical type of physics or things like that, so I don't like this dirty world.

A:

What is your goal as a politician or chancellor? What did you want to achieve as chancellor of Germany?

MERKEL'S G.S.:

My aim is to make the world one organization, for world peace, of course.

A:

One organization?

MERKEL'S G.S.:

Yeah, the EU is the first step. And the next step is a world organization more powerful than the United Nations as it is.

A:

That seems like totalitarianism.

---

*Weeks after this spiritual interview, Chancellor Merkel announced her resignation as the leader of CDU on October 29, 2018. She intends to continue her chancellorship until the end of the term in fall 2021, but will retire from politics after that.

MERKEL'S G.S.:

Oh, no, no, not so. No, no, no, no. All countries are equal and independent, but they can argue about their serious problems in a common place, public place, and after their deliberately... they made... deliberately they make... hmm... furious, no, no, no... why is English so difficult... favorly, or... no, no, no... urgently... no, no... arguing... arguing very much, they can make a conclusion. At that time, they should obey the conclusion of the members. That is not totalitarianism, I think.

C:

How do you view President Trump's recent speech at the United Nations? Because he stressed the importance of the sovereignty of each country many times.

MERKEL'S G.S.:

Uh huh, he's a gunman, so he wants to do as he likes. He's threatening the world. It's his way of cowboy. In some meaning, such kind of person is required at the time of crisis, but in the usual period, we must have good conversations. He is too much self-concentrated person. If we can have more power, I mean the EU power, we can have an equal conversation with him, but he has a strong power, so it's difficult. He's dividing the world now and he wants to go back to the age of wars, the war era of the Middle Age. Now is the day of democracy. He doesn't understand democracy. He just wants to be a champion. So, that's the problem.

C:

But Trump's position was to respect each country's independence. And they...

MERKEL'S G.S.:

No, no. It's a performance. No, no.

C:

He really wants each country to bear responsibility for their own prosperity.

MERKEL'S G.S.:

Yeah, yeah, yeah, it's true. It's true.

C:

I think that sounds reasonable. What do you think of his stance?

MERKEL'S G.S.:

All countries must be or should be equal, but the strengths, I mean the political strength, economic strength and the strength of leaders are quite different. All are not equal as it is. So, we must have some kind of, how do I say, some kind of help for weaker countries, weaker leaders, and countries of poverty. He doesn't think about that. His "America-First" policy, in some meaning, will be successful for the American people, but in another meaning, it will destroy the world order.

2

Views on Trump, Xi Jinping, and Putin

M:

Now, you seem to have a severe attitude or severe stance toward President Trump of the United States. So, how can you manage the relationship between the United States and Germany or the EU?

MERKEL'S G.S.:

The United States, it's in New York, so they are under the control of the United... ah, the United Nations are under the control of the United States of America, so it's not neutral, I think. America's enemy is an enemy of the United Nations. We need balance. The balance is, one is of course the United States and another one is of course the EU, and the third one might be the Asian power. The Asian power logically leads to the conclusion that it must be made by Japan and China. In the near future, the African power must be added to that.

M:

How will you make a good relationship between the United States of America and the EU?

MERKEL'S G.S.:

Firstly, Mr. Donald Trump must learn that American law is not the world law or common law in the meaning of cosmopolitanism and international law. American law is not international law. It's also the same for China. China's inner law is not international law. Xi Jinping doesn't understand this truth. Both Xi Jinping and Donald Trump, and adding to that, Russian Putin. He also cannot understand. Russian rule is the world rule, he thinks so. These dictatorships must have a chance to learn about the world; world geographic studying and the main rule of international law. They have *Defekt* ("flaw" in German) in that point. They don't have enough common law in them.

I said common law, it's an easy saying, but in another meaning, my common law is a law of conscience and of course the law of God. God is not assisting the United States only. God assists all the world, all the countries of the world, so Donald Trump can say instead of the American people the profit of the United States, but it's not enough. It's one part of the common law. Another common law is required to help other countries and other nations of other religions which they belong to. They are lacking. So, even if they have divine nature and charismatic personality, they are tribe-level gods, small "g" gods, I think.

M:

Thank you. Since you referred to the world leaders, could you tell us what you think of President Xi Jinping of China and President Putin of Russia?

MERKEL'S G.S.:

Xi Jinping is a difficult person, I think. If you want to make him an enemy, it's easy to make him angry and that will make a new war in the near future. But he's very kind to his friends. He has two characters in him, so we need some kind of comprehension between Xi Jinping and us, the world leaders. He's a difficult person.

But if you study deep into the world history, number-one-China era covered almost half of the world, I think, especially in these 2,000 years. So, we must think that the age of China is coming in the near future, more than 50 percent level. We must stand that kind of age. But in another situation, we can control China under the name of the United Nations or under the name of relationship between the EU, Japan, the United States, and Russia. And you added Vladimir Putin?

M:

Yes.

MERKEL'S G.S.:

Ah, hmm. He's one of the dictators, I think. His dictatorship is very skillful, so I appreciate him in his skill, but his understanding of democracy is maybe 50 percent or so. He must learn a lot from other democratic countries. He is from KGB, so he has a very suspicious mind in him. He cannot rely on other countries. He is apt to think that they are enemies, so it's a problem. It's like China. But I had several conversations with him and he's a very smart guy. He can think and he can make new rules by himself. So, the country Russia can be made in any direction if he wants. The importance is the intelligence which he gets from other leaders of the world, I think. The isolation of Russia is not so good. But we are now making economic sanctions with the United States, the EU, and Japan, so he's being isolated, but it's a not-so-good direction.

3
Can We Change the Regime of China, a Country of No God?

A:

You said the United Nations and the United States, Japan, and the EU can control China. Does that mean we can change the Chinese regime?

MERKEL'S G.S.:

[*Clicks tongue.*] Ah, it's difficult. They lack the concept of God. That's a problem. Xi Jinping is God. Yeah, of course in our histories, God himself appeared in human history, but in the area of politics, it's very dangerous, I think. God who has human nature can be acceptable in our histories, but usually, he or she must be a strong leader in the mindset-changers meaning. The practical political power is not the condition of God and the existence of God's power itself. This political power must be made from the gathered power of people.

A:

What do you think of the oppression to religious groups in China, such as Christians and Muslims? What do you think of the violation of human rights in China?

MERKEL'S G.S.:

[*Sighs.*] It's difficult. Communist one-party system denies God and religion. They think of religion as LSD or a drug-like thing. In another meaning, they think of religion as a mind-controller, the spring of mind-controllers. So, religious leaders can mind-control their people and it will usually confront with political power and make confusion and conflict. That is the reason he doesn't like religions. It's from the history of China. In the history of China, sometimes there occurred a political revolution, but in anytime, it occurred from religious leaders. This is their own conditions, so it's difficult to persuade him. He is, for example, afraid of... how do you say... "Horinko" group (Falun Gong), or Christian groups of China. They have more than one hundred million population. It's over the communist members in China. It's difficult to deal with, so he is fearing religious groups. You, Happy Science will be next.

A:

Germany has been building a good economic relationship with China, but in a spiritual message from Jesus Christ, he said, "Which do you like, money or God?"*

MERKEL'S G.S.:

Of course, money.

A:

"Of course, money"? [*Laughs.*]

MERKEL'S G.S.:

Yeah. God said, "Love poverty." So, he's evil.

A:

But you said you believe in God.

---

* On September 25, 2018, three days before this spiritual interview, the author conducted a Q&A session titled, "Jesus Christ's Answers In English" at Happy Science General Headquarters. It was a session where Jesus Christ answered questions in the form of a spiritual message. In the session, one of the interviewers asked Jesus about the strengthening economic ties between Germany and atheist China, to which he first replied, "Which do you like, money or God?"

MERKEL'S G.S.:

Uh huh. Wealthy God is good. It's a meaning of Protestant, you know?

M:

It's true. It's true.

MERKEL'S G.S.:

It's true.

C:

How do you see President Trump's policy of imposing tariffs on the Chinese economy? Because it seems that he wants to make the Chinese economy weaker in order to stop military expansion.

MERKEL'S G.S.:

Umm, the effect will be half and half. In some meaning, it has influence, of course, but in another meaning, it will make the people of the world poorer and poorer because they must pay more money to buy common things, like food, cars, other electronic tools, or something. So, it's not so good for people.

M:

What do you think of President Xi Jinping's plan, the One Belt One Road Initiative?

MERKEL'S G.S.:

Hmm, it's his ambition. If he were a god, it will be a good policy. If he were a satan, it's not good. Its "road" means his aim to make the countries surrender to him, the countries which are beside or on the belt or road. He wants to conquer these countries. If he were a satan, it's not good. If he were a god, it's a good thing. It depends. [*Laughs.*]

M:

Do you think President Xi is a god or a satan?

MERKEL'S G.S.:

Maybe an ordinary person.

M:

Oh. So, you see President Xi as just an ordinary person.

MERKEL'S G.S.:

Ordinary person, but has a strength in will. Thinking-and-realizing-his-dream power is strong. It belongs to both god and satan.

M:

Germany seems to support the Chinese plan, I mean, President Xi's One Belt One Road initiative. Am I correct?

MERKEL'S G.S.:

Yeah because he, or China, has been buying a lot of Mercedes-Benz.

We got profit from China. So, we are not losing, we got money from China. But China will make inner-side economy to buy and sell the Mercedes-Benz and... I don't know about that. I have no concern about that. *Ich habe nichts zu tun* ("I have nothing to do" in German) about that. But as a country-to-country relationship, we made good profit. So, it's not so bad.

A:

Last year, Master Ryuho Okawa pointed out that it's possible that the EU and China will collapse at the same time.

MERKEL'S G.S.:

Hahahaha, oh, no, no, no!

A:

What is your outlook?

MERKEL'S G.S.:

No, no. At the same time!? Who wants to do that? Trump?

A:

Yes, Trump is aiming to make the Chinese economy collapse.

MERKEL'S G.S.:

He will fall in the next election.

A:

What is your outlook about the Chinese economy?

MERKEL'S G.S.:

Hmm... Now, they are in the situation of a trade war, I mean between the United States and China. Both will lose in the conclusion. So, I'm afraid the world economic recession will occur from this conflict. It can.

M:

You studied physics at university. And some people criticize that you don't have much knowledge or understanding about economics.

MERKEL'S G.S.:

Of course, that's right. That's right.

M:

Do you agree?

MERKEL'S G.S.:

I agree. I don't have much concern about that. But I can read the figure only. It's black or red. OK. I can read the figures of the conclusion of the B/S (balance sheet).

M:

So, your basic or fundamental understanding of economics is black or red?

MERKEL'S G.S.:

Yeah, that's right.

M:

Is that all?

MERKEL'S G.S.:

Yeah. Yeah, my physical legal mind says so.

4

Any Good Policies for the German Economy?

C:

Master Okawa said that unless Germany is strong in the EU, the EU will not prosper. So, I think the German economy is very important. Do you have any good economic policies?

MERKEL'S G.S.:

Oh, I'm too kind to weaker people. I have too much intention to rescue the refugees from Africa and Syria, and the Turkish people. So, they say that will make the German economy weaker and weaker. They say so. But I have conscience within me, so it's beyond economy. I must help them. I'm simply thinking that I get a lot of money from China and use it to help refugees. That's all. Very smart and simple.

M:

Yes. It's very simple.

C:

But when an economic crisis happened... when the Greek debt crisis happened in 2010, your country didn't really help.

MERKEL'S G.S.:

Oh, I'm a physicist, so at that time I will leave this position, so I have no problem.

A:

You strongly insist on instituting an austerity policy on other countries in the EU. That makes negative impact on the EU economy.

MERKEL'S G.S.:

What do you mean by negative impact? I can't understand your English. What is negative impact?

A:

Many other countries don't have enough budget, so they can't manage their economy.

MERKEL'S G.S.:

But I say that every country like Greece—it's a small and weak economy they have—all of them must stand up by themselves. I said so. They said it's too cold or unfriendly, but I learned this philosophy from Master Ryuho Okawa, so it's correct, I think.

C:

With regard to your immigrant policy, I learned recently that about one-fifth of the people in Germany are immigrants from other countries. So, that's why many right wing parties, such as AfD, Alternative für Deutschland, emerged, becoming powerful. What do you think of this kind of populist movement in Germany?

MERKEL'S G.S.:

Hmm. In some meaning, it was predictable. But I am the love of the world [*laughs*], so I must help weaker people. Master Okawa will come soon to Deutschland, oh, Germany, and he will say the same thing. "To help the people of the world, the poor people, that is the mission of religion. So, Happy Science will supply a lot of money to Germany," he will say so. "I will bring a lot of money from Japan to Germany," he will say so, he must say so.

C:

I think one of the reasons your party's supporting rate is declining is because of your policy on immigrants. Do you think you have to reflect upon your immigrant policy in order to gain more power of your party?

MERKEL'S G.S.:

Uh huh. To tell the truth, I, myself as a human, I like to live poor. It leads to the intellectual life, I think. Gaining money too much makes people weaker in their brain thinking. So, too much money is a poison, in reality, in my heart.

M:

Are you saying you hate wealth deep in your mind?

MERKEL'S G.S.:

In reality, I'm not a politician. I think like a physicist, so I don't like secular problems. Donald Trump is a very secular person, you know? He is good at earning money and using money and playing with girls, like that, buy land and sell land and build buildings and sell them. He is good at these kinds of secular matters. But to tell the truth, I don't like those kinds of matters. I just want to think.

5

Where Did Nazism Come From?

M:

OK. You mentioned that you have conscience. So, you want to help poor people. Is it related to the German history, I mean Nazism?

MERKEL'S G.S.:

Oh, I'm quite contrary to Nazism. I hate it. I hate Nietzscheism, I hate Heidegger, and I also hate Hegelian. These kinds of thoughts have made totalitarian system or supported totalitarian system. You usually say, "It's a mistake of Karl Marx," but it's from Hegelian philosophy. Next were Nietzsche and Heidegger. So, German philosophies made totalitarianism and Hegel's godlike philosophy produced the chosen-people thought in Germany and it made anti-Semitism, I mean the anti-Jewish people-ism. Anti-Semitism comes from this kind of Hegelian and Nietzschean thoughts.

C:

Is there any philosopher you admire?

MERKEL'S G.S.:

Hmm. Buddha is not so bad. He is not a philosopher, but it's not so bad. Jesus Christ has a problem, of course. If he lived in these days, he would be a refugee, Turkish people- or Syrian people- or Egyptian people- or Libyan people-like person, maybe. No goods, no money, and beg for food.

M:

I think Germany is prosperous in the economic meaning, but Germany doesn't have a central pole in mentality or philosophy. What kind of philosophy or thinking idea...

MERKEL'S G.S.:

No, no. We don't need such kind of central pole. From the starting point, Martin Luther of Protestantism said, "Don't belong to churches. Don't belong to the Roman Catholic or one Pope. You, yourself belong to God through reading the German translation of the New Testament. Please read the German-translated New Testament and belong to God by oneself, in each family." That is the starting point of our religion, so everyone is independent in this meaning. We don't need "one-pole system"-like thinking.

6
"My Dream in the Next Century is 'a Global-Level Government'"

A:

What kind of vision do you have for the future of the EU or Germany?

MERKEL'S G.S.:

To tell the truth, I'm not so strong at building new economy. I was born in West Germany, but brought up in East Germany. So I, myself suffered a lot of influence from the old-fashioned Russian style of politics and economy. So, it's very difficult. I'm not a Donald Trump-like person, so I am not so good at selling and buying. Before me, there was Margaret Thatcher in the U.K. She was good at buying and selling because she was a girl of a small store, but I am not. So, I have a dream and a theory, but it's very pure and so people cannot follow me, I think. But my dream will come true in the next century. I hope so.

C:

What is your dream?

MERKEL'S G.S.:

"Gather a lot of nations and have conversations and make decisions and follow them. And every country, every nation is equal, but they all believe in God and hate war" system is essential.

A:

Who will be your God at that time?

MERKEL'S G.S.:

Oh. The God of the Earth.

A:

So, you mean we should have one government in the next century?

MERKEL'S G.S.:

Hmm, that expression is misleading, so... We must think about a global-level government. It's not the one-party system of communists. It's quite different. We need conversations. We must reflect a lot of opinions from other countries. But the problem is, if one country has one vote, the weaker countries have a lot of members, so in the economic meaning, it is unprofitable for stronger countries in economy like Japan or the United States or the U.K. or Germany or France, like those countries.

A:

Do you mean the United Nations will transform into a world government?

MERKEL'S G.S.:

Hmm, it would be one possibility. But to tell the truth, the United Nations lacks the budget and the leaders of first level, or topflight leaders because the leader of the United Nations is selected from third countries, I mean not great countries, for example, South Korea. Not the president or the prime minister, but the foreign minister-level people will be elected. So, their management power is not so high. It's a problem. The American president usually looks down upon the secretary-general of the United Nations. Maybe he or she will come from the weak countries, a foreign minister-level person.

C:

What do you think of the concept of sovereignty? Because Brexit happened: many British people wanted to make their country's decisions on their own. That's really the issue here.

MERKEL'S G.S.:

It's not so good. It's isolationism and a self-concentrated thinking like Donald Trump's. They are keeping their own money. They are afraid of getting rid of their money, from them to weaker countries of the EU or other countries of Africa or Islamic countries. So, the United Kingdom is running away from the EU with their money. But it means too much burden on Germany and France. It's a beginning of the collapse of the EU.

C:

So, you mean the concept of sovereignty or nationalism is not important anymore?

MERKEL'S G.S.:

Hmm, in some meaning, it's important. Sovereignty or nationality is important. Managing the EU is very difficult. I have been feeling difficulties in many languages and of course the traditions and cultures of every nation. So, from the beginning it was forecast to be very difficult. But we must resist against this kind of confusion. We must conquer this confusion. We can learn from each other. The German people, to tell the truth, don't like the French people, and of course the U.K. people, the United States people, and the Russian people and, in addition to that, they don't like the Japanese people. These are strong countries in economy, and of course, in the military meaning. So, we cannot sleep well if they were getting stronger and stronger.

C:

But due to the globalization, your country also lost jobs. The gap between the haves and have-nots is increasing in Germany as well. So, what do you think of this situation in Germany?

MERKEL'S G.S.:

Oh, at that time, I want to study physics and reading books and hiking and have fun listening to classical music. I worked a lot. It's enough. So, it's the next person who carries the burden from other countries. It's beyond my power.

7

What Merkel's Guardian Spirit Thinks of National Security

M:

I would like to ask you about your view of military power. Since you hate war, you don't want war. Of course, we don't want war, but some people said, "We can stop war because we have defensive power." Do you agree with it?

MERKEL'S G.S.:

In the theoretical thinking, if the United States abandons budget for their arms, it will help the poverty of all over the world. They can. But at the same time, there needs the abandonment of armed forces of China and Russia. At that time, if Russia abandoned that kind of arming budget, the EU can reduce such kind of budget and these budgets can be used for the purpose of helping poor people of the world. Almost billions of people are lacking food every day, so we can help them. We will teach them, for example the African people, the technology for peacemaking and how they can make their own revenue of the nation and budget. At that time we want to say to them, "Be independent." So, military budget reduction, I mean, make it fewer and fewer is essential for the time being, I think.

M:

How can you persuade the world leaders to abandon their military power?

MERKEL'S G.S.:

The bottleneck is Hitler's thing. We can't say too much about that. They, meaning the countries surrounding us, usually say, "You are the most dangerous country." They say so. "You produced Adolf Hitler and destroyed the world," so we don't have enough opinion about that. We are in the same situation like Japan in this meaning. But now is the day to reconsider about that. Adolf Hitler was born in Austria, so [*laughs*] it's not Germany.

A:

But President Trump is proposing that Germany should increase its military budget to two to four percent of the GDP. What do you think of that proposal?

MERKEL'S G.S.:

Donald Trump is good at thinking money, so I hate him. We don't need any money for defending our country. Love peace and love God. That's cheap.

M:

But I think the Western countries fear Russia because Russia was their enemy in the Cold War, so...

MERKEL'S G.S.:

Yeah, enemy. Yeah, indeed enemy.

M:

So, if you want to protect your country and the EU, I think you need NATO. But you don't want to support the NATO system?

MERKEL'S G.S.:

Ah, the NATO system [*clicks tongue*]. It costs a lot. Main target is Russia, so [*clicks tongue*] it's difficult. Russia has a lot of nuclear weapons, so NATO must protect themselves from Russia. We chose China to earn money and to make a balance between Russia and the EU. If we have a good relationship with China, then the EU and China can protect us from Russia.

M:

Perhaps, are you thinking that the EU and China will have an alliance between them?

MERKEL'S G.S.:

China is far from Europe, so we don't think it's dangerous. But Russia did a lot to the EU, European countries. Sometimes Napoleon attacked Russia, but was ruined. Hitler attacked Russia, but was ruined. They are strong and in every time, they have been enemies of Europe. They have an expansionist idea. They need non-frozen sea, that's the reason, I think so. Give your northern islands to them, including Hokkaido. They will be happy. They can use the ocean.

8
Merkel's Past Life—
A Great Philosopher Who Sought
For Perpetual Peace

M:

I'd like to ask you about your spiritual secret.

MERKEL'S G.S.:

Oh. Spiritual secret. Hmm.

M:

Before this session began, Master Okawa said "today will be an astonishing day." What do you think he means?

MERKEL'S G.S.:

Hmm. It means I'm not she, I'm not he. I'm human.

M:

That means you are an existence beyond the sexes or genders?

MERKEL'S G.S.:

No, no, no.

M:

What do you mean?

MERKEL'S G.S.:

Hahahaha. Yeah, Angela Merkel is a lady now. But her guardian spirit is a man.

M:

So, you are a male.

MERKEL'S G.S.:

Yeah, male.

M:

If possible, could you reveal your name, please?

MERKEL'S G.S.:

Oh, you know. You know my name, of course. All the Japanese know my name.

M:

Could you give us a tip or hint? In which era?

MERKEL'S G.S.:

I'm a philosopher.

C:

Kant?

MERKEL'S G.S.:

Ah, Immanuel Kant. So, I'm not so good at economy. You know?

M:

So, Immanuel Kant is reborn as Chancellor Angela Merkel.

MERKEL'S G.S.:

Yeah, true.

M:

Yeah, it's an astonishing fact. It is.

MERKEL'S G.S.:

Yeah. Your Master predicted so. I have already published my spiritual books in your group. So, I also am a guiding spirit of Happy Science.

M:

Ah, I see. Master said you can speak Japanese, too.

MERKEL'S G.S.:

Yeah, of course.

M:

So, that means...

MERKEL'S G.S.:

Hanaseruyo ("I can speak" in Japanese), of course.

M:

[*Laughs.*] No, please speak in English this time.

MERKEL'S G.S.:

I'm *hikari no tenshi ne. Dakara nihongo shabereru ne* ("an angel of light, so I can speak Japanese" in Japanese).

[*Interviewers and audience laugh.*]

MERKEL'S G.S.:

I can speak Japanese because I'm an angel of light.

M:

That means you once were a Japanese? You were once born in Japan? Is it...

MERKEL'S G.S.:

In Japan? Hmm... No, I'm a European, I have been. But Japanese people learned a lot from me.

M:

Yes. We studied...

MERKEL'S G.S.:

Yeah, Meiji period, Taisho period, and Showa period. And now nothing to learn from me.

A:

Your purpose of being born in this age is to make peace in Europe?

MERKEL'S G.S.:

I am the origin of the thinking to build up the United Nations, and the small United Nations is the EU, so I appeared.

A:

You want a world government in the next century?

MERKEL'S G.S.:

Yeah, a Kant-like government. We are confronted with the issue of China. You dislike China and have a containing-China policy. But I have an idea of how to steal from China in terms of money. So, we are Dracula to get blood from China.

M:

So now, Germany is stealing wealth from China?

MERKEL'S G.S.:

Yeah, yeah. Today, they want Mercedes-Benz or Germans' very developed technologies or goods, so they admire Germany. But it will make them modernized and westernized. And at the tipping point, they will change. Karl Marx is not a good German, but his influence is still in China. So, they have respect for Germany. Their political thinking is from Karl Marx, so we will change China at the tipping point. So, never mind. I can, we can change China. Japan already studied Kant's philosophy. It's old-fashion now, but it's really made modern Japanese thinking methods, so at that time, Japan can be a leader of China.

A:

I think President Trump and Chancellor Merkel can cooperate with each other. That will make the world prosperous and peaceful.

MERKEL'S G.S.:

He is a man of sex, but I am a man of philosophy.

M:

But President Trump was President George Washington, the first president, in one of his past lives.*

MERKEL'S G.S.:

Really? Oh, really? He's a very poor farmer.

M:

[*Laughs.*] Yes, but President Trump helps Lord El Cantare's ideas and plans, so please help him and…

MERKEL'S G.S.:

Ah, he should study more. He cannot understand Kant's philosophy, so he needs more talented brain. He must be reborn again.

A:

If you want to be in power for a few more years, you should cooperate with him.

---

* Spiritual investigations by Happy Science have revealed that President Trump was George Washington in his past life. See Chapters 3 and 4 in Ryuho Okawa, *The Trump Secret: Seeing Through the Past, Present, and Future of the New American President* (New York: IRH Press, 2017).

MERKEL'S G.S.:

I know. Of course, I can be the teacher of Donald Trump, but he will not hear me. He's a bad student, so he never will.

M:

OK. The time is almost up, so lastly, could you give a message to the people of Germany and the EU?

MERKEL'S G.S.:

Oh, OK. [*Sighs.*] Please remember. You, modern Japanese people owe a lot from Germany and now is the time to return it to Germany. Thank you very much. [*Laughs.*]

M:

OK, thank you very much.

MERKEL'S G.S.:

Mou iika ne? ("Is that enough?" in Japanese.)

[*Audience laugh.*]

MERKEL'S G.S.:

Mou, eigo wa tsukareru wa ("It's tiresome to speak in English" in Japanese.) *Mou iika ne?* OK?

M:

Yoroshii desu ka? Hai. Saigo ni, sousai sensei ga kondo Doitsu ni ikaremasu keredomo, nanika, ossharitaikoto toka arimasuka? ("Is that OK? OK. Lastly, Master is going to Germany, so do you have anything to say to him?" in Japanese.)

MERKEL'S G.S.:

Please praise Angela Merkel. "She is the greatest lady in the world, this century." If your Master said so, it's enough.

M:

OK, thank you very much.

MERKEL'S G.S.:

Thank you. [*Claps once.*]

A:

Thank you very much.

MERKEL'S G.S.:

Bye.

Chapter SEVEN

Spiritual Interviews with the Guardian Spirit of Donald Trump (Excerpts)

Recorded on August 29, 2017 & April 28, 2018
at Happy Science General Headquarters
Tokyo, Japan

1

Donald Trump's Guardian Spirit Speaks on His Strategy Against China (August 29, 2017)

My main point is to end Chinese totalitarianism

O:

If your strategy succeeds, China will be under big threat from you, and then China will allow you to govern the whole peninsula with South Korea. Is that right?

DONALD TRUMP'S GUARDIAN SPIRIT:

[*Sighs.*] OK. Xi Jinping is one of my friends. When he relies on and hears my words correctly, he is my good friend. If he disregards my saying, it is the beginning of his collapse, I mean, he will lose his political power in the near future.

America, the United States is quite different. I am not Obama. Obama will lose, but I'll never lose. I can save Japan. I can save South Korea. If some people survive after our attack, I will save such kind of North Korean people.

Of course, I'll change China's strategy for the future. They will make their gear change into the Western type of democracy. This is my main point. The attack on North Korea will change them. I think so. They are totalitarianism. China, also, is like that, so totalitarianism of the Chinese also must be changed from Xi Jinping regime to Hong Kong-like regime.

O:
Don't you think that, after the Kim Jong-un regime, China will intervene in building a new nation in the Korean Peninsula?

TRUMP'S G.S.:
No, no, no. No possibility. They cannot win against our strategic military force. We have thousands of missiles or ICBMs, but they have only 400... It's just defensive ones, defensive missiles. But we have thousands of missiles. We can destroy all over China. It's impossible.

The Chinese economy is on the palm of my own

I:
About the future of North Korea, do you have any agreement under the table with China?

TRUMP'S G.S.:
No.

I:
How about Russia? Did you talk to Mr. Putin about North Korea?

TRUMP'S G.S.:

Russia is a very small... smaller country in the economic meaning and they only just show their political power using military power, but the end of the military power of Russia is coming soon. The starting point is the ruins of North Korea. I will destroy the military powers of China and Russia, also. Both of them.

The world should be led by us, the United States. We are the country of God and we have great reliance between Japan and the U.S., so we will make a new age as Mr. Ryuho Okawa said already, we will lead the next 300 years with our freedom and democratic system, and of course the liberalism within. We can make the world wealthier and make the happiness greater.

O:

On the other hand, you have another big issue. You have a huge trade deficit with China, so you have to deal with this issue as well.

TRUMP'S G.S.:

It's OK, no problem. It's OK. At any time, we can make the deficit smaller than now because if we can be the top leader of the world, we can change the system, of course. For example, the foreign exchange rate, how to use the tariff system, or how to make the United Nations or other organizations. It depends on me. So, I can handle easily the Chinese economy. They are on the palm of my own.

O:

So, China will have to face huge pressure from your administration, right?

TRUMP'S G.S.:

Yeah. That is the reason I appeared as a president of the U.S.

The U.S. and Japan can make a new world

A:

What is your strategy to end the totalitarian state of China?

TRUMP'S G.S.:

Firstly, the miserable result of North Korea will lead them to change their future. That kind of "military first" system is old-fashioned. It's the end of the Mao Zedong thinking. So, China should change and they should believe in God. That is my aim and my main point. China needs a new God or religion, an orthodox religion. They need religion. They need love for the world and peace for the world.

They need fairness in the rule of their trade and in using the intellectual rights. I mean, they easily steal the wisdom of other countries, technologies or things like that. So, they must be fair in the near future. That is the standpoint of a great country. They must be changed. They must be educated. I already started to change the world.

O:

I think you are right, but I still didn't understand why the past U.S. presidents didn't take that strategy against China.

TRUMP'S G.S.:

Because they are weak people. I'm not so weak. I, myself, feel that I can hear the thinking or emotion of God. So, I'm the representative of God, I think.

Mr. Ryuho Okawa made a path to the future, so I will just run through this way. We, I mean the U.S. and Japan, Donald Trump and Ryuho Okawa, are the best alliances of the world. We can make, remake the new world.

The North Korean problem is not more than a hurricane. It's OK. I will deal with it and I'll settle it. You can rely on us.

2

Spreading Freedom Throughout the World
(April 28, 2018)

What is the first strategy to a world full of democracy?

K:

Good morning, Mr. Trump. I just came back from the United States three months ago. We, Happy Science, have been counting on you...

TRUMP'S G.S.:

I know, I know, I know.

K:

...the biggest example being Master Ryuho Okawa coming to New York and giving a lecture, where he told people, "Mr. Trump will be the president,"* and it was realized.

TRUMP'S G.S.:

Thank you.

---

* On October 2, 2016, the author gave a lecture in English, "Freedom, Justice, and Happiness" at Crowne Plaza Times Square Manhattan in New York. See Chapter 2 in the aforementioned *The Trump Secret: Seeing Through the Past, Present, and Future of the New American President.*

K:

Thank you so much for your decisions and solutions on political issues. As a result, the U.S. economy is getting better and better.

What I'd like to ask is, looking at the situation in the world, Xi Jinping of China and Putin of Russia are ruling their countries as dictators. I believe you are the protector of democracy. What do you see in the future? How would you deal with this situation to make the world full of democracy?

TRUMP'S G.S.:

The first strategy is that we must strengthen the treaty between the U.S. and Japan. This is the first strategy. I hope Mr. Abe, or Mr. Abe-like statesman, will lead Japan continuously and we, the two countries, can protect against evil to keep the real democratic system. This is the first thing.

Next is the relationship between the U.S. and the EU. We must keep good ties with the EU because Putin of Russia, I know his ability, but these days, he's changing a little. You said dictatorship. Yeah, really, he has dictatorship. It sometimes means the enemy of democratic system. We need elections.

Of course, Russia has election systems, but in the real meaning, the conclusion is predicted because no one can conquer military power. So, Putin will continue his strong-style dictatorship. He's thinking about rebounding as a superpower. Russia, again, wants to become a superpower. He's trying to protect against the EU because in the EU, several countries have long-distance missiles made by the

U.S.A. So, he's very serious about that.

At this point, Syria is the most difficult country. It's the main point of the struggle between the U.S.A. and Russia. It means the Assad regime. How do you think about that? What do you think of the Assad regime? Is this correct or not? He has justice or not? If he is evil, we must destroy his regime. But Russia, they have a friendship between the two countries. There is friendship, so Putin will never forgive our attack. Our attack means, for example, the attack of the U.S., the French, and the U.K.

So, the most difficult problem is if Russia, China, North Korea and South Korea, if these four countries want to have some kind of treaty in the military meaning, at that time, Japan and the United States, we two must fight against them. It would trigger Third World War. So, diplomacy is quite, quite difficult from now on, I think.

K:

Do you think Abe can handle the situation?

TRUMP'S G.S.:

I'm the guardian spirit, but we must respect the friendship and personality of Mr. Abe, so I can't say the real thing. Please forgive me about that.

He is a good man. He's continuously seeking for Japanese peace. He has confidence in the United States; its democratic policy and military power. He relies on us, so we want to keep good friendship with him. It's difficult to speak frankly, but to tell the truth, he has nothing to do now. He is at a loss. He is not counted in the world politics today. He is, how do I say, he has a little weak will, I guess.

Trump's thoughts on the unification of Koreas

I:

Thinking about the unification of North and South Koreas, do you agree on the unification of North and South Koreas? Or, do you have any opinions about the Korean Peninsula?

TRUMP'S G.S.:

As you already insisted, we must support South Korea. South Korean regime should prevail on North Korea. This kind of unification is permissible. But if North Korea has super-power over South Korea, I cannot admit that situation. So, the conclusion is freedom, equality, no dictatorship, especially military dictatorship, and election system.

A:

The intention of the two, Kim Jong-un and Moon Jae-in, is to create unification on an equal footing. Can you accept that?

TRUMP'S G.S.:

It is a weakness of Moon Jae-in, but I cannot control his character.

I, myself, have stronger opinion and attitude toward Kim Jong-un, but in the meantime, I must show, or we must show, a welcoming attitude toward peace-making activities for the world.

If we can have a conversation and if, by dint of conversation only, we can denuclearize the Korean Peninsula, and if we can accept the proposal of Mr. Abe, the future will be better. But in reality, we won't have such kind of positive future. We are preparing for the worst situation.

A:

The unification of the South and North means the withdrawal of the U.S. troops from the Korean Peninsula. What do you think of that?

TRUMP'S G.S.:

Impossible. Impossible. They, meaning the North Korean military government, will lose their power; this is the conclusion, there is no other choice. They must admit that they are losers. We are not losers and we are not equal. They must know about that. If possible, I can destroy North Korea within three days. We are not equal. They should know that.

But South Korean Moon Jae-in, he is a little weak. If his conversation attitude means that, before his next visit to Pyongyang, he will aid a lot of materials, food and energy to North Korea as a gift, if he is that weak, we will take a more and more strong attitude. I mean, we will go back to the starting point.

I:

You said Mr. Moon is weak.

TRUMP'S G.S.:

Weak.

I:

From your viewpoint, what kind of person is he? What do you think about his character?

TRUMP'S G.S.:

Moon Jae-in? Just Korean.

I:

Just Korean? What do you expect of him in this matter?

TRUMP'S G.S.:

[*Sighs.*] There's one possibility. He wants to solve the problem in a Korean way of thinking. But we, historically, analyze that these kinds of activities have been mistakes every time. So, he will lose in conversation and negotiation with Kim Jong-un.

Mr. Kim Jong-un is never a peace-maker. He's never a peace-maker. He is the maker of dangerous situations around the east part of Asia. So, he must apologize to South Korean people,

Japanese people, and other Asian countries. He should appreciate the cooperation of China and appreciate my smile, I think. He's a bad guy.

I:
You said dangerous situations in the Korean Peninsula. So, what...

TRUMP'S G.S.:
He made it.

I:
Can you foresee the future dangerous situations in East Asia?

TRUMP'S G.S.:
Uh huh. Kim Jong-un is thinking that they want to use the power of China and they want to make a balance of power between China and the United States. But now, his analysis is just a mistake. Chinese Xi Jinping thinks that now, they cannot have military collision with us because China cannot win in that war. If China, Russia, North and South Korea, these four countries have conglomerate power on us, and we lose the relationship between Japan and the United States, at that time, their chance will be 50-50. But now, China doesn't like to make trouble with us, so it's difficult for him.

K:

We are learning Master Ryuho Okawa's teachings, and one of them says that what's happening in the spiritual world will be realized in this world. So, if Mr. Trump will meet Mr. Kim Jong-un in person in the future, did you, as a guardian spirit, already meet Kim Jong-un's guardian spirit in the spiritual world?

TRUMP'S G.S.:

Ah. As you know, I'm one of the gods of the United States. He is not a god, but he is a dictator of North Korea. He is one of the members of Satans in North Korea. I know about that. So, we cannot be real friends.

"After the North Korean problem, I will try changing China"

A:

Could you tell us about the strategy against China? You have started the trade war. What is your intention and what will happen in the near future against China?

TRUMP'S G.S.:

They have a large population, but each Chinese person cannot be like an American. So, they have their limits. Because Chinese government has surveillance on their own people. As you said already, they have in the real meaning, no religious freedom and, of course, no political freedom. Only economic freedom, they insist. But this is a bad system. So, I want to change it.

We believe in the power of every person, I mean, the people of the nation. Democracy has its aim. Its aim is to let the people be happier. But in China, people are suppressed by a dictatorship-like government.

So, our next struggle or war just began. I will change China. This is the next step. If I'm permitted the next presidency, I mean, eight years as a president of the United States, the four years I have left will be to change the political system and the religious system of China. How to change their system including the trade system. So, please rely on me. After I end the North Korean problem, I will try changing China and, of course, changing Russia.

A:
You always say that Xi Jinping is a very good man and that you love him [*laughs*].

TRUMP'S G.S.:
Xi Jinping is a good person in reality, like Kim Jong-un now.

[*Audience laughs.*]

A:

I understand.

TRUMP'S G.S.:

Yeah, a good person. Haha. I have a business mind, so please forgive me.

I:

Now, China is expanding like hegemony in the Pacific area. I heard that they're going to divide the Pacific Ocean into two at the Hawaiian Islands. We heard that they have a very evil intention.

TRUMP'S G.S.:

Uh huh, OK. But Japan will win if Japan can only again compete with China. I hope so. Japan will regain power and compete with China in these 20 or 30 years in the future. I'm not so pessimistic about that.

Oh, OK. We reign within the Hawaiian area. But another area of the Pacific Rim will be controlled by the country of Japan. It's OK. It's enough. I believe in Japanese people. You will succeed again.

I:

Thank you very much for your trust in Japan.

K:

Economically, I think you will still keep an "America First" policy and strengthen the U.S. economy and fulfill a mission. What is your ideal image of East Asia in the future? How do you see the relationship between East Asia and the United States?

TRUMP'S G.S.:

East Asia... I'm thinking East Asia, West Asia, Africa, the EU, and all over the world. It's the position of the president of the United States. I'm thinking about all the world, the Earth, every day. I think about everything. When I want to attack Syria, on the same day, I want to attack North Korea and on the same day, I want to attack Iran.

Can you understand? This is the position or power of the president of the United States.

"Liberty should lead to prosperity and happiness"

A:

Could you tell us about the idea of liberty because you, President Trump, sometimes say, "liberty comes from our Creator."

TRUMP'S G.S.:

We are struggling or fighting against countries where liberty is lost or suppressed by dictatorship, like old-style Russia, China, North Korea, Islamic people and some African countries. And of course, the countries which are controlled under the power of gigantic China. So, liberty should lead to the future prosperity and the happiness of the people.

What we should do can be easily found in the area where there is no liberty. That's our job and our mission from God. Americanization should include the mission of God.

But there also occur religious conflicts and they are very difficult to settle. So, the power would be the power of Happy Science. You need more power than Islam, Christianity or Chinese-like no-God system. You need billions of members. Please fight against your enemies and get more members. I hope so.

The problem and limit of the EU

I:

Moving to the EU, Europe, I heard you met President Macron of France. What do you think about him?

TRUMP'S G.S.:

Oh, yeah, a good man. He's a good man, also. [*Laughs.*] He's a good man. Good man, yeah, good man. Yeah. That's it.

I:

How about Merkel, German Chancellor Merkel?

TRUMP'S G.S.:

[*Sighs.*] A little problem... problem. She has a little problem. She might be a cancer of the EU. She is not a dictator, but her influence, political influence is too big in the EU. But she comes from East

Germany, so in her brain, there is some kind of old-fashioned Soviet-like thinking or Chinese-like thinking. So, she's logical, but I'm afraid that she doesn't get the real meaning of economic freedom or political freedom.

The EU has its limit. There are a lot of countries to be saved, but there is no strong country that can save them, so the United Kingdom wants to say goodbye to the EU. It has its reason. So, this problem is very difficult.

Macron is a micron [*audience laughs*]. Oh, misfire. Macron… Macron, please change your wife. New model car like me. I changed to a younger wife and I got new source of ideas. He will be expected to marry a younger woman than he is and it will make a new idea, a new wave in Europe.

Merkel already ended her mission. It just means there is no reliable person in the EU. So, America must watch all over the EU.

I:

Thank you very much. Soon, we have to conclude today's session. For the last message, could you show some strong card in your hand to the world? Do you have any secret or plan about politics, economy, or any other matters?

TRUMP'S G.S.:

To Japanese people, please rely on me. Don't abandon Mr. Abe at this moment.

I'm reaching China, not to be helped by China, but I'm aiming at changing China soon as the next problem after North Korea. I already understand the problem.

Please work in the U.S.A., "Trump should continue his presidency. He needs four more years. The next president should be Donald Trump. He is younger than he is. He is like 60 years old in power and cleverness." If you are doing activities like that, I love you so much.

I:

Mr. President, thank you very much for today's session. Thank you very much.

TRUMP'S G.S.:

Say hello to your followers all over the world. Thank you.

I:

Thank you very much.

RYUHO OKAWA

[*Claps twice.*]

This book is a compilation of the lectures and spiritual interviews as listed below.

PART I: LECTURE
- Chapter One -
Love for the Future + Q&A
Lecture given on October 7, 2018
at The Ritz-Carlton, Berlin, Germany

- Chapter Two -
The Fact and the Truth + Q&A
Lecture given on May 22, 2011
at Kowloonbay International Trade & Exhibition Centre, Hong Kong

- Chapter Three -
Love Beyond Hatred + Q&A

Japanese title: *Ai wa Nikushimi wo Koete*
Lecture given on March 3, 2019
at Grand Hyatt Taipei, Taipei, Taiwan

Further Reading:
Excerpt from
"The Realization of Buddhaland Utopia"

Japanese title: *Bukkokudo Utopia no Jitsugen*
Lecture given on March 3, 2008
at Taipei Local Temple, Happy Science, Taipei, Taiwan

PART II: SPIRITUAL INTERVIEW

- Chapter Four -

Spiritual Interview with
the Guardian Spirit of Xi Jinping (Excerpt)

Japanese title: *Shugorei Interview Xi Jinping Sekai Shihai e no Scenario*

Recorded on June 21, 2018

at Special Lecture Hall, Happy Science, Tokyo, Japan

- Chapter Five -

Spiritual Interview with
the Guardian Spirit of Vladimir Putin (Excerpt)

Japanese title: *Nichiro Heiwa Joyaku ga Tsukuru Shin Sekai Chitsujo Putin
Daitoryo Shugorei Kinkyu Message*

Recorded on November 9, 2018

at Special Lecture Hall, Happy Science, Tokyo, Japan

- Chapter Six -

Spiritual Interview with
the Guardian Spirit of Angela Merkel (Excerpt)

Recorded on September 28, 2018

at Special Lecture Hall, Happy Science, Tokyo, Japan

- Chapter Seven -

Spiritual Interviews with
the Guardian Spirit of Donald Trump (Excerpts)

Recorded on August 29, 2017 & April 28, 2018

at General Headquarters, Happy Science, Tokyo, Japan

ABOUT THE AUTHOR

Ryuho Okawa was born on July 7th 1956, in Tokushima, Japan. After graduating from the University of Tokyo with a law degree, he joined a Tokyo-based trading house. While working at its New York headquarters, he studied international finance at the Graduate Center of the City University of New York. In 1981, he attained Great Enlightenment and became aware that he is El Cantare with a mission to bring salvation to all of humankind. In 1986 he established Happy Science. It now has members in over 100 countries across the world, with more than 700 local branches and temples as well as 10,000 missionary houses around the world. The total number of lectures has exceeded 2,900 (of more than 130 are in English) and over 2,500 books (of more than 500 are Spiritual Interview Series) have been published, many of which are translated into 31 languages. Many of the books, including *The Laws of the Sun* have become best seller or million seller.

Up to date, Happy Science has produced 18 movies. These projects were all planned by the executive producer, Ryuho Okawa. Recent movie titles are *Hikari au Inochi – Kokoro ni Yorisou 2 –* (literally, "Our Lives Shine Together – Heart to Heart 2 –," documentary to be released Aug. 2019), *Immortal Hero* (live-action movie to be released Oct. 2019), and *Shinrei Kissa EXTRA no Himitsu – The Real Exorcist –* (literally, "The Secret of Spirits' Café EXTRA – The Real Exorcist –," live-action movie to be released in 2020). He has also composed the lyrics and music of over 100 songs, such as theme songs and featured songs of movies. Moreover, he is the Founder of Happy Science University and Happy Science Academy (Junior and Senior High School), Founder and President of the Happiness Realization Party, Founder and Honorary Headmaster of Happy Science Institute of Government and Management, Founder of IRH Press Co., Ltd., and the Chairperson of New Star Production Co., Ltd. and ARI Production Co., Ltd.

WHAT IS EL CANTARE?

El Cantare means "the Light of the Earth," and is the Supreme God of the Earth who has been guiding humankind since the beginning of Genesis. He is whom Jesus called Father, and His branch spirits, such as Buddha and Hermes, have descended to Earth many times and helped to flourish many civilizations. To unite various religions and to integrate various fields of study in order to build a new civilization on Earth, a part of the core consciousness has descended to Earth as Master Ryuho Okawa.

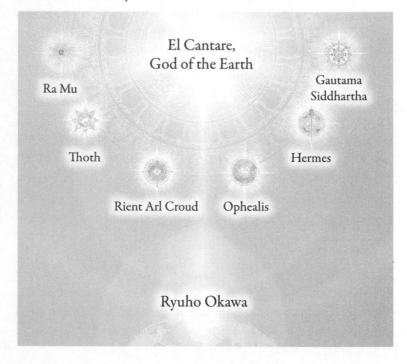

El Cantare,
God of the Earth

Ra Mu

Gautama
Siddhartha

Thoth

Hermes

Rient Arl Croud   Ophealis

Ryuho Okawa

Buddha
Gautama Siddhartha was born as a prince into the Shakya Clan in India around 2,600 years ago. When he was 29 years old, he renounced the world and sought enlightenment. He later attained Great Enlightenment and founded Buddhism.

Hermes
In the Greek mythology, Hermes is thought of as one of the 12 Olympian gods, but the spiritual Truth is that he taught the teachings of love and progress around 4,300 years ago that became the origin of the rise of the Western civilization. He is a hero that truly existed.

Ophealis
Ophealis was born in Greece around 6,500 years ago and was the leader who took an expedition to as far as Egypt. He is the God of miracles, prosperity, and arts, and is known as Osiris in the Egyptian mythology.

Rient Arl Croud
Rient Arl Croud was born as a king of the ancient Incan Empire around 7,000 years ago and taught about the mysteries of the mind. In the heavenly world, he is responsible for the interactions that take place between various planets.

Thoth
Thoth was an almighty leader who built the golden age of the Atlantic civilization around 12,000 years ago. In the Egyptian mythology, he is known as god Thoth.

Ra Mu
Ra Mu was a leader who built the golden age of the civilization of Mu around 17,000 years ago. As a religious leader and a politician, he ruled by uniting religion and politics.

WHAT IS A SPIRITUAL MESSAGE?

We are all spiritual beings living on this earth. The following is the mechanism behind Master Ryuho Okawa's spiritual messages.

1 You are a spirit

People are born into this world to gain wisdom through various experiences and return to the other world when their lives end. We are all spirits and repeat this cycle in order to refine our souls.

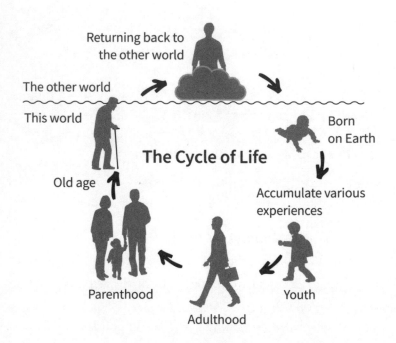

Returning back to the other world

The other world

This world

Born on Earth

The Cycle of Life

Old age

Accumulate various experiences

Parenthood

Adulthood

Youth

2 You have a guardian spirit

Guardian spirits are those who protect the people who are living on this earth. Each of us has a guardian spirit that watches over us and guides us from the other world. They were us in our past life, and are identical in how we think.

The other world

This world

Watches over us/
sends us inspiration

3 How spiritual messages work

Master Ryuho Okawa, through his enlightenment, is capable of summoning any spirit from anywhere in the world, including the Spirit World.

Master Okawa's way of receiving spiritual messages is fundamentally different from that of other psychic mediums who undergo trances and are thereby completely taken over by the spirits they are channeling. Master Okawa's attainment of a high level of enlightenment enables him to retain full control of his consciousness and body throughout the duration of the spiritual message. To allow the spirits to express their own thoughts and personalities freely, however, Master Okawa usually softens the dominancy of his consciousness. This way, he is able to keep his own philosophies out of the way and

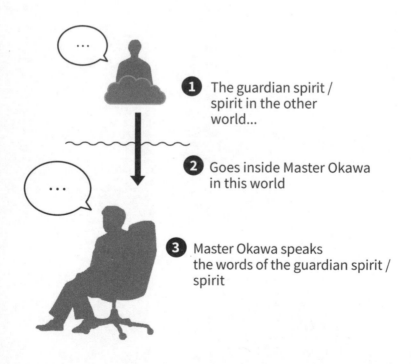

1 The guardian spirit / spirit in the other world...

2 Goes inside Master Okawa in this world

3 Master Okawa speaks the words of the guardian spirit / spirit

ensure that the spiritual messages are pure expressions of the spirits he is channeling.

Since guardian spirits think at the same subconscious level as the person living on earth, Master Okawa can summon the spirit and find out what the person on earth is actually thinking. If the person has already returned to the other world, the spirit can give messages to the people living on earth through Master Okawa.

For more about spiritual messages and a complete list of books in the Spiritual Interview Series, visit okawabooks.com

ABOUT HAPPY SCIENCE

Happy Science is a global movement that empowers individuals to find purpose and spiritual happiness and to share that happiness with their families, societies, and the world. With more than twelve million members around the world, Happy Science aims to increase awareness of spiritual truths and expand our capacity for love, compassion, and joy so that together we can create the kind of world we all wish to live in.

Activities at Happy Science are based on the Principles of Happiness (Love, Wisdom, Self-Reflection, and Progress). These principles embrace worldwide philosophies and beliefs, transcending boundaries of culture and religions.

Love teaches us to give ourselves freely without expecting anything in return; it encompasses giving, nurturing, and forgiving.

Wisdom leads us to the insights of spiritual truths, and opens us to the true meaning of life and the will of God (the universe, the highest power, Buddha).

Self-Reflection brings a mindful, nonjudgmental lens to our thoughts and actions to help us find our truest selves—the essence of our souls—and deepen our connection to the highest power. It helps us attain a clean and peaceful mind and leads us to the right life path.

Progress emphasizes the positive, dynamic aspects of our spiritual growth—actions we can take to manifest and spread happiness around the world. It's a path that not only expands our soul growth, but also furthers the collective potential of the world we live in.

PROGRAMS AND EVENTS

The doors of Happy Science are open to all. We offer a variety of programs and events, including self-exploration and self-growth programs, spiritual seminars, meditation and contemplation sessions, study groups, and book events.

Our programs are designed to:
* Deepen your understanding of your purpose and meaning in life
* Improve your relationships and increase your capacity to love unconditionally
* Attain peace of mind, decrease anxiety and stress, and feel positive
* Gain deeper insights and a broader perspective on the world
* Learn how to overcome life's challenges
   ... and much more.

*For more information, visit **happy-science.org**.*

INTERNATIONAL SEMINARS

Each year, friends from all over the world join our international seminars, held at our faith centers in Japan. Different programs are offered each year and cover a wide variety of topics, including improving relationships, practicing the Eightfold Path to enlightenment, and loving yourself, to name just a few.

HAPPY SCIENCE MONTHLY

Happy Science regularly publishes various magazines for readers around the world. The Happy Science Monthly, which now spans over 300 issues, contains Master Okawa's latest lectures, words of wisdom, stories of remarkable life-changing experiences, world news, and much more to guide members and their friends to a happier life. This is available in many other languages, including Portuguese, Spanish, French, German, Chinese, and Korean. Happy Science Basics, on the other hand, is a 'theme-based' booklet made in an easy-to-read style for those new to Happy Science, which is also ideal to give to friends and family. You can pick up the latest issues from Happy Science, subscribe to have them delivered (see our contacts page) or view them online.*

* Online editions of the *Happy Science Monthly* and
Happy Science Basics can be viewed at:
info.happy-science.org/category/magazines/

*For more information, visit **www.happy-science.org***

WEBSITE

HAPPY SCIENCE OFFICIAL WEBSITE

Happy Science's official website introduces the organization's founder and CEO, Ryuho Okawa, as well as Happy Science teachings, books, lectures, temples, the latest news, and more.

happy-science.org

HAPPY SCIENCE UNIVERSITY

THE FOUNDING SPIRIT AND THE GOAL OF EDUCATION

Based on the founding philosophy of the university, "Exploration of happiness and the creation of a new civilization," education, research and studies will be provided to help students acquire deep understanding grounded in religious belief and advanced expertise with the objectives of producing "great talents of virtue" who can contribute in a broad-ranging way to serve Japan and the international society.

FACULTIES

FACULTY OF HUMAN HAPPINESS

Students in this faculty will pursue liberal arts from various perspectives with a multidisciplinary approach, explore and envision an ideal state of human beings and society.

FACULTY OF SUCCESSFUL MANAGEMENT

This faculty aims to realize successful management that helps organizations to create value and wealth for society and to contribute to the happiness and the development of management and employees as well as society as a whole.

FACULTY OF FUTURE CREATION

Students in this faculty study subjects such as political science, journalism, performing arts and artistic expression, and explore and present new political and cultural models based on truth, goodness and beauty.

FACULTY OF FUTURE INDUSTRY

This faculty aims to nurture engineers who can resolve various issues facing modern civilization from a technological standpoint and contribute to the creation of new industries of the future.

HAPPY SCIENCE ACADEMY
JUNIOR AND SENIOR HIGH SCHOOL

Happy Science Academy Junior and Senior High School is a boarding school founded with the goal of educating the future leaders of the world who can have a big vision, persevere, and take on new challenges.

Currently, there are two campuses in Japan; the Nasu Main Campus in Tochigi Prefecture, founded in 2010, and the Kansai Campus in Shiga Prefecture, founded in 2013.

Nasu Main Campus   Kansai Campus

HAPPINESS REALIZATION PARTY

The Happiness Realization Party (HRP) was founded in May 2009 by Master Ryuho Okawa as part of the Happy Science Group to offer concrete and proactive solutions to the current issues such as military threats from North Korea and China and the long-term economic recession. HRP aims to implement drastic reforms of the Japanese government, thereby bringing peace and prosperity to Japan. To accomplish this, HRP proposes two key policies:

1) Strengthening the national security and the Japan-U.S. alliance which plays a vital role in the stability of Asia.

2) Improving the Japanese economy by implementing drastic tax cuts, taking monetary easing measures and creating new major industries.

HRP advocates that Japan should offer a model of a religious nation that allows diverse values and beliefs to coexist, and that contributes to global peace.

*For more information, visit **en.hr-party.jp***

SOCIAL CONTRIBUTIONS

Happy Science tackles social issues such as suicide and bullying, and launches heartfelt, precise and prompt rescue operations after a major disaster.

◆ **The HS Nelson Mandela Fund**

The Happy Science Group provides disaster relief and educational aid overseas via this Fund. We established it following the publication of *Nelson Mandela's Last Message to the World*, a spiritual message from the late Nelson Mandela, in 2013. The fund actively provides both material and spiritual aid to people overseas—support for victims of racial discrimination, poverty, political oppression, natural disasters, and more.

Examples of how the fund has been used:

Provided tents in rural Nepal

Supplied food and water immediately after the Nepal earthquake

Donated a container library to South African primary school, in collaboration with Nelson Mandela Foundation

◆ **We extend a helping hand around the world to aid in post-disaster reconstruction and education.**

Nepal: After the 2015 Nepal Earthquake, we promptly offered our local temple as a temporary evacuation center and utilized our global network to send water, food and tents. We will keep supporting their recovery via the HS Nelson Mandela Fund. In addition, we have collaborated with the Nepalese Ambassador in Japan to offer a portion of the profit from the movie, *The Rebirth of Buddha* (see p.277), to build schools and provide educational support in Nepal, the birthplace of Buddha.

Sri Lanka: Provided aid in constructing school buildings damaged by the tsunami. Further, with the help of the Sri Lankan prime minister, 100 bookshelves were donated to Buddhist temples.

India: Ongoing aid since 2006—uniforms, school meals, etc. for schools in Bodh Gaya, a sacred ground for Buddhism. Medical aid in Calcutta, in collaboration with local hospitals.

China: Donated money and tents to the Szechuan Earthquake disaster zone. Books were also donated to elementary schools in Gansu Province, near the disaster zone.

Malaysia: Donated money, educational materials and clothes to local orphanages. Relief supplies were sent to areas in northeast Malaysia, site of the 2015 floods.

Thailand: Constructed libraries and donated books to elementary and junior high schools damaged by floods in Ayutthaya.

Indonesia: Donated to the Sumatra-Andaman Earthquake disaster zone.

The Philippines: Donated books and electric fans to elementary schools on Leyte Island in July 2015. Provided aid in the aftermath of Typhoon Haiyan (Yolanda) and donated 5,000 sets of health and hygiene kits.

Uganda: Donated educational materials and mosquito nets to protect children from malaria. Offered scholarships to orphans diagnosed with AIDS.

Kenya: Donated English copies of Happy Science books, *Invincible Thinking*, *An Unshakable Mind* and *The Laws of Success* to schools. (Designated as supplementary text by the Kenyan Ministry of Education in July 2014.)

Ghana: Provided medical supplies as a preventive measure against Ebola.

South Africa: Collaborated with the Nelson Mandela Foundation in South Africa to donate a container library and books to an elementary school.

Australia: Donated to the flood-affected northeastern area in 2011 via the Australian Embassy.

New Zealand: Donated to the earthquake-stricken area in February 2011 via the New Zealand Embassy.

Iran: Donated to the earthquake-stricken area in northeastern Iran in October 2012 via the Iranian Embassy.

Brazil: Donated to the flood-affected area in January 2011.

OTHER ACTIVITIES

Happy Science does other various activities to provide support for those in need.

- ◆ **You Are An Angel!**
  General Incorporated Association
  Happy Science has a volunteer network in Japan that encourages and supports children with disabilities as well as their parents and guardians.

- ◆ **Never Mind School for Truancy**
  At 'Never Mind,' we support students who find it very challenging to attend schools in Japan. We also nurture their self-help spirit and power to rebound against obstacles in life based on Master Okawa's teachings and faith.

- ◆ **"Prevention against suicide" campaign since 2003**
  A nationwide campaign to reduce suicides; over 20,000 people commit suicide every year in Japan. "The Suicide Prevention Website-Words of Truth for You-" presents spiritual prescriptions for worries such as depression, lost love, extramarital affairs, bullying and work-related problems, thereby saving many lives.

- ◆ **Support for anti-bullying campaigns**
  Happy Science provides support for a group of parents and guardians, Network to Protect Children from Bullying, a general incorporated foundation launched in Japan to end bullying, including those that can even be called a criminal offense. So far, the network received more than 5,000 cases and resolved 90% of them.

DOCUMENTARY MOVIE
HEART TO HEART

In this documentary movie, Happy Science University students visit these NPO activities to discover what salvation truly is, and on the meaning of life, through heart to heart interviews.

- **The Golden Age Scholarship**
  This scholarship is granted to students who can contribute greatly and bring a hopeful future to the world.

- **Success No.1**
  Buddha's Truth Afterschool Academy
  Happy Science has over 180 classrooms throughout Japan and in several cities around the world that focus on afterschool education for children. The education focuses on faith and morals in addition to supporting children's school studies.

- **Angel Plan V**
  For children under the age of kindergarten, Happy Science holds classes for nurturing healthy, positive, and creative boys and girls.

- **Future Stars Training Department**
  The Future Stars Training Department was founded within the Happy Science Media Division with the goal of nurturing talented individuals to become successful in the performing arts and entertainment industry.

- **New Star Production Co., Ltd.**
  ARI Production Inc.
  We have companies to nurture actors and actresses, artists, and vocalists. They are also involved in film production.

MOVIE NEWS

Up to date, Happy Science has produced 18 movies. These projects were all planned by and the original stories were written by the executive producer and director, Ryuho Okawa. Our movies have received various awards and recognition around the world.

....

The animation movie, *The Laws of the Universe – Part I*, released simultaneously in Japan and the U.S. in October 2018, has received a total of 5 awards from 4 countries (as of May, 2019). We thank you all for your support, and we wish that this movie can spread even more and people can discover this one and only Truth taught at Happy Science.

5 Awards from **4** Countries!

France
on
May 18th

NICE INTERNATIONAL FILM FESTIVAL 2019
BEST INTERNATIONAL ANIMATION AWARD

U.K.
on
May 25th

LONDON INTERNATIONAL MOTION PICTURE AWARDS 2019
BEST INTERNATIONAL ANIMATION FEATURE FILM AWARD

India

CALCUTTA INTERNATIONAL CULT FILM FESTIVAL
[OUTSTANDING ACHIEVEMENT AWARD]

U.S.

FILM INVASION LOS ANGELES
[GRAND JURY PRIZE – BEST ANIME FEATURE]

AWARENESS FILM FESTIVAL
[SPECIAL JURY ANIMATION AWARD]

Lineup of Happy Science Movies

Discover the spiritual world you have never seen and
Come close to the Heart of God through these movies.

•1994•
The Terrifying Revelations
of Nostradamus
(Live-action)

•1997•
Love Blows Like the Wind
(Animation)

•2000•
The Laws of the Sun
(Animation)

•2003•
The Golden Laws
(Animation)

•2006•
The Laws of Eternity
(Animation)

•2009•
The Rebirth of Buddha
(Animation)

•2012•
The Final Judgement
(Live-action)

•2012•
The Mystical Laws
(Animation)

•2015•
The Laws of the Universe - Part 0
(Animation)

•2016•
I'm Fine, My Angel
(Live-action)

•2017•
The World We Live In
(Live-action)

•2018•
Heart to Heart
(Documentary)

•2018•
DAYBREAK
(Live-action)

•2018•
The Laws of the Universe - Part I
(Animation)

•2019•
The Last White Witch
(Live-action)

•2019•
Heart to Heart 2
(Documentary)

—— Coming Soon ——

•2019•
Immortal Hero
(Live-action)

Contact your nearest local branch for more information on how to watch HS movies.

CONTACT INFORMATION

Happy Science is a worldwide organization with faith centers around the globe. For a comprehensive list of centers, visit the worldwide directory at *happy-science.org*. The following are some of the many Happy Science locations:

UNITED STATES AND CANADA

New York
79 Franklin St.,
New York, NY 10013
Phone: 212-343-7972
Fax: 212-343-7973
Email: ny@happy-science.org
Website: happyscience-na.org

San Francisco
525 Clinton St.,
Redwood City, CA 94062
Phone & Fax: 650-363-2777
Email: sf@happy-science.org
Website: happyscience-na.org

New Jersey
725 River Rd, #102B,
Edgewater, NJ 07020
Phone: 201-313-0127
Fax: 201-313-0120
Email: nj@happy-science.org
Website: happyscience-na.org

Los Angeles
1590 E. Del Mar Blvd.,
Pasadena, CA 91106
Phone: 626-395-7775
Fax: 626-395-7776
Email: la@happy-science.org
Website: happyscience-na.org

Florida
5208 8thSt., Zephyrhills,
FL 33542
Phone: 813-715-0000
Fax: 813-715-0010
Email: florida@happy-science.org
Website: happyscience-na.org

Orange County
10231 Slater Ave. #204
Fountain Valley, CA 92708
Phone: 714-745-1140
Email: oc@happy-science.org
Website: happyscience-na.org

Atlanta
1874 Piedmont Ave. NE, Suite 360-C
Atlanta, GA 30324
Phone: 404-892-7770
Email: atlanta@happy-science.org
Website: happyscience-na.org

San Diego
7841 Balboa Ave., Suite #202
San Diego, CA 92111
Phone: 619-381-7615
Fax: 626-395-7776
E-mail: sandiego@happy-science.org
Website: happyscience-na.org

Hawaii
Phone: 808-591-9772
Fax: 808-591-9776
Email: hi@happy-science.org
Website: happyscience-na.org

Toronto
845 The Queensway
Etobicoke, ON M8Z 1N6 Canada
Phone: 1-416-901-3747
Email: toronto@happy-science.org
Website: happy-science.ca

Kauai
4504 Kukui Street.,
Dragon Building Suite 21,
Kapaa, HI 96746
Phone: 808-822-7007
Fax: 808-822-6007
Email: kauai-hi@happy-science.org
Website: happyscience-na.org

Vancouver
#212-2609 East 49th Avenue
Vancouver, BC, V5S 1J9, Canada
Phone: 1-604-437-7735
Fax: 1-604-437-7764
Email: vancouver@happy-science.org
Website: happy-science.ca

INTERNATIONAL

Tokyo
1-6-7 Togoshi, Shinagawa
Tokyo, 142-0041 Japan
Phone: 81-3-6384-5770
Fax: 81-3-6384-5776
Email: tokyo@happy-science.org
Website: happy-science.org

Sydney
516 Pacific Hwy, Lane Cove North,
NSW 2066, Australia
Phone: 61-2-9411-2877
Fax: 61-2-9411-2822
Email: sydney@happy-science.org
Website: happyscience.org.au

London
3 Margaret St.
London,W1W 8RE United Kingdom
Phone: 44-20-7323-9255
Fax: 44-20-7323-9344
Email: eu@happy-science.org
Website: happyscience-uk.org

South Sao Paulo
Rua. Domingos de Morais 1154,
Vila Mariana, Sao Paulo
SP-CEP 04010-100, Brazil
Phone: 55-11-5574-0054
Fax: 55-11-5088-3806
Email: sp_sul@happy-science.org
Website: happyscience.com.br

Jundiai
Rua Congo, 447, Jd. Bonfiglioli
Jundiai-CEP, 13207-340, Brazil
Phone: 55-11-4587-5952
Email: jundiai@happy-science.org

Uganda
Plot 877 Rubaga Road, Kampala
P.O. Box 34130, Kampala, Uganda
Phone: 256-79-3238-002
Email: uganda@happy-science.org

Seoul
74, Sadang-ro 27-gil,
Dongjak-gu, Seoul, Korea
Phone: 82-2-3478-8777
Fax: 82-2- 3478-9777
Email: korea@happy-science.org

Thailand
19 Soi Sukhumvit 60/1,
Bang Chak, Phra Khanong,
Bangkok, 10260 Thailand
Phone: 66-2-007-1419
Email: bangkok@happy-science.org
Website: happyscience-thai.org

Taipei
No. 89, Lane 155, Dunhua N. Road.,
Songshan District, Taipei City 105,
Taiwan
Phone: 886-2-2719-9377
Fax: 886-2-2719-5570
Email: taiwan@happy-science.org

Indonesia
Darmawangsa
Square Lt. 2 No. 225
Jl. Darmawangsa VI & IX
Indonesia
Phone: 021-7278-0756
Email: indonesia@happy-science.org

Malaysia
No 22A, Block 2, Jalil Link Jalan
Jalil Jaya 2, Bukit Jalil 57000, Kuala
Lumpur, Malaysia
Phone: 60-3-8998-7877
Fax: 60-3-8998-7977
Email: malaysia@happy-science.org
Website: happyscience.org.my

Philippines Taytay
LGL Bldg, 2nd Floor,
Kadalagaham cor,
Rizal Ave. Taytay,
Rizal, Philippines
Phone: 63-2-5710686
Email: philippines@happy-science.org

Nepal
Kathmandu Metropolitan City
Ward No. 15, Ring Road, Kimdol,
Sitapaila Kathmandu, Nepal
Phone: 977-1-427-2931
Email: nepal@happy-science.org

ABOUT IRH PRESS

IRH Press Co., Ltd, based in Tokyo, was founded in 1987 as a publishing division of Happy Science. IRH Press publishes religious and spiritual books, journals, magazines and also operates broadcast and film production enterprises. For more information, visit *okawabooks.com*.

Follow us on:

Facebook: Okawa Books

Twitter: Okawa Books

Goodreads: Ryuho Okawa

Instagram: OkawaBooks

Pinterest: Okawa Books

The Laws Series is an annual volume of books that are mainly comprised of Ryuho Okawa's lectures on various topics that highlight principles and guidelines for the activities of Happy Science every year. *The Laws of the Sun*, the first publication of the laws series, ranked in the annual best-selling list in Japan in 1994. Since then, all of the laws series' titles have ranked in the annual best-selling list for more than two decades, setting socio-cultural trends in Japan and around the world.

THE TRILOGY

The first three volumes of the Laws Series, *The Laws of the Sun*, *The Golden Laws*, and *The Nine Dimensions* make a trilogy that completes the basic framework of the teachings of God's Truths. *The Laws of the Sun* discusses the structure of God's Laws, *The Golden Laws* expounds on the doctrine of time, and *The Nine Dimensions* reveals the nature of space.

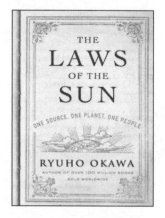

THE LAWS OF THE SUN

One Source, One Planet, One People

Paperback • 288 pages • $15.95
ISBN: 978-1-942125-43-3

IMAGINE IF YOU COULD ASK GOD why He created this world and what spiritual laws He used to shape us—and everything around us. If we could understand His designs and intentions, we could discover what our goals in life should be and whether our actions move us closer to those goals or farther away.

At a young age, a spiritual calling prompted Ryuho Okawa to outline what he innately understood to be universal truths for all humankind. In *The Laws of the Sun*, Okawa outlines these laws of the universe and provides a road map for living one's life with greater purpose and meaning.

In this powerful book, Ryuho Okawa reveals the transcendent nature of consciousness and the secrets of our multidimensional universe and our place in it. By understanding the different stages of love and following the Buddhist Eightfold Path, he believes we can speed up our eternal process of development. *The Laws of the Sun* shows the way to realize true happiness—a happiness that continues from this world through the other.

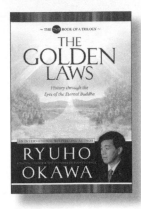

THE GOLDEN LAWS

History through the Eyes of the Eternal Buddha

Paperback • 216 pages • $14.95
ISBN: 978-1-941779-81-1

Throughout history, Great Guiding Spirits of Light have been present on Earth in both the East and the West at crucial points in human history to further our spiritual development. *The Golden Laws* reveals how Divine Plan has been unfolding on Earth, and outlines 5,000 years of the secret history of humankind. Once we understand the true course of history, through past, present and into the future, we cannot help but become aware of the significance of our spiritual mission in the present age.

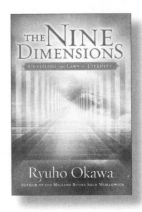

THE NINE DIMENSIONS

Unveiling the Laws of Eternity

Paperback • 168 pages • $15.95
ISBN: 978-0-982698-56-3

This book is a window into the mind of our loving God, who designed this world and the vast, wondrous world of our afterlife as a school with many levels through which our souls learn and grow. When the religions and cultures of the world discover the truth of their common spiritual origin, they will be inspired to accept their differences, come together under faith in God, and build an era of harmony and peaceful progress on Earth.

THE LAWS OF JUSTICE

How We Can Solve World Conflicts and Bring Peace

Paperback • 208 pages • $15.95
ISBN: 978-1-942125-05-1

This book shows what global justice is from a comprehensive perspective of the Supreme God. Becoming aware of this view will let us embrace differences in beliefs, recognize other peoples divine nature, and love and forgive one another. It will also become the key to solving the issues we face, whether they are religious, political, societal, economic, or academic, and help the world become a better and safer world for all of us living today.

THE TRUMP SECRET

Seeing Through the Past, Present, and Future
of the New American President

Paperback • 208 pages • $14.95
ISBN: 978-1-942125-22-8

Donald Trump's victory in the 2016 presidential election surprised almost all major vote forecasters who predicted Hillary Clinton's victory. But 10 months earlier, in January 2016, Ryuho Okawa, Global Visionary, a renowned spiritual leader, and international best-selling author, had already foreseen Trump's victory. This book contains a series of lectures and interviews that unveil the secrets to Trump's victory and makes predictions of what will happen under his presidency. This book predicts the coming of a new America that will go through a great transformation from the "red and blue states" to the United States.

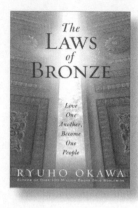

THE LAWS OF BRONZE

Love One Another, Become One People

Paperback • 224 pages • $15.95
ISBN: 978-1-942125-50-1

With the advancement of science and technology leading to longer life-span, many people are seeking out a way to lead a meaningful life with purpose and direction. This book will show people from all walks of life that they can solve their problems in life both on an individual level and on a global scale by finding faith and practicing love. When all of us in this planet discover our common spiritual origin revealed in this book, we can truly love one another and become one people on Earth.

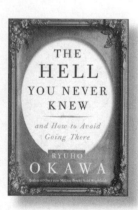

THE HELL YOU NEVER KNEW

and How to Avoid Going There

Paperback • 208 pages • $15.95
ISBN: 978-1-942125-52-5

From ancient times, people have been warned of the danger of falling to Hell. But does the world of Hell truly exist? If it does, what kind of people would go there? Through his spiritual abilities, Ryuho Okawa found out that Hell is only a small part of the vast Spirit World, yet more than half of the people today go there after they die. Okawa believes the true mission of religion is to save the souls of all people, and eventually, dissolve the world of Hell. That is why he gives the detailed description about the Spirit World, including Heaven and Hell, and encourage people to choose the right path.

THE STRONG MIND

The Art of Building the Inner Strength
to Overcome Life's Difficulties

Paperback • 192 pages • $15.95
ISBN: 978-1-942125-36-5

In this book, Ryuho Okawa shares his personal
experiences as examples to show how we can
build toughness of the heart, develop richness
of the mind, and cultivate the power of
perseverance. The strong mind is what we need
to rise time and again, and to move forward no
matter what difficulties we face in life. This book
will inspire and empower you to take courage,
develop a mature and cultivated heart, and
achieve resilience and hardiness so that you can
break through the barriers of your limits and
keep winning in the battle of your life.

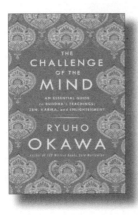

THE CHALLENGE OF THE MIND

An Essential Guide to Buddha's Teachings:
Zen, Karma and Enlightenment

Paperback • 208 pages • $16.95
ISBN: 978-1-942125-45-7

In this book, Ryuho Okawa explains essential
Buddhist tenets and how to put these ideas
into practice. Enlightenment is not just an
abstract idea but one that everyone can experience to some extent. In clear but thought-
provoking language, Okawa imbues new life
into traditional teachings and offers a solid
basis of reason and intellectual understanding
to often overcomplicated Buddhist concepts.
By applying these basic principles to our lives,
we can direct our minds to higher ideals and
create a bright future for ourselves and others.

THE ART OF INFLUENCE

28 Ways to Win People's Hearts and Bring Positive Change to Your Life

Paperback • 264 pages • $15.95
ISBN: 978-1-942125-48-8

Ryuho Okawa offers 28 questions he received from people who are aspiring to achieve greater success in life. At times of trouble, setback, or stress, these pages will offer you the inspirations you need at that very moment and open a new avenue for greater success in life. The practiced wisdom that Okawa offers in this book will enrich and fill your heart with motivation, inspiration, and encouragement.

WORRY-FREE LIVING

Let Go of Stress and Live in Peace and Happiness

Hardcover • 192 pages • $16.95
ISBN: 978-1-942125-51-8

We can cultivate peace of mind and attain inner happiness in life, even as we go through life's array of difficult experiences. The wisdom Ryuho Okawa shares in this book about facing problems in human relationships, financial hardships, and other life's stresses will help you change how you look at and approach life's worries and problems for the better. Let this book be your guide to finding precious meaning in all your life's problems, gaining inner growth no matter what you face, and practicing inner happiness and soul-growth all throughout your life.

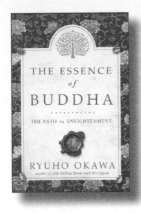

THE ESSENCE OF BUDDHA
The Path to Enlightenment

Paperback • 208 pages • $14.95
ISBN: 978-1-942125-06-8

In this book, Ryuho Okawa imparts in simple and accessible language his wisdom about the essence of Shakyamuni Buddha's philosophy of life and enlightenment–teachings that have long been inspiring people all over the world for over 2,500 years. By offering a new perspective on core Buddhist thoughts that have long been cloaked in mystique, Okawa brings these teachings to life for modern people. *The Essence of Buddha* distills a way of life that anyone can practice to achieve a life of self-growth, compassionate living, and true happiness.

MESSAGES FROM HEAVEN
What Jesus, Buddha, Moses, and Muhammad Would Say Today

Hardcover • 224 pages • $19.95
ISBN: 978-1-941779-19-4

If you could speak to Jesus, Buddha, Moses, or Muhammad, what would you ask? In this book, Ryuho Okawa shares the spiritual communication he had with these four spirits and the messages they want to share with people living today. The Truths revealed in this book will open your eyes to a level of spiritual awareness, salvation, and happiness that you have never experienced before.

MY JOURNEY THROUGH THE SPIRIT WORLD
A True Account of My Experiences of the Hereafter

THE LAWS OF FAITH
One World Beyond Differences

THE LAWS OF INVINCIBLE LEADERSHIP
An Empowering Guide for Continuous and
Lasting Success in Business and in Life

THE STARTING POINT OF HAPPINESS
An Inspiring Guide to Positive Living with Faith, Love, and Courage

INVINCIBLE THINKING
An Essential Guide for a Lifetime of Growth, Success, and Triumph

THE LAWS OF MISSION
Essential Truths for Spiritual Awakening in a Secular Age

HEALING FROM WITHIN
Life-Changing Keys to Calm, Spiritual, and Healthy Living

THE UNHAPPINESS SYNDROME
28 Habits of Unhappy People (and How to Change Them)

THE LAWS OF SUCCESS
A Spiritual Guide to Turning Your Hopes Into Reality

A LIFE OF TRIUMPH
Unleashing Your Light Upon the World

THE MIRACLE OF MEDITATION
Opening Your Life to Peace, Joy, and the Power Within

THE HEART OF WORK
10 Keys to Living Your Calling

THINK BIG!
Be Positive and Be Brave to Achieve Your Dreams

INVITATION TO HAPPINESS
7 Inspirations from Your Inner Angel

SECRETS OF THE EVERLASTING TRUTHS
A New Paradigm for Living on Earth

THE MOMENT OF TRUTH
Become a Living Angel Today

CHANGE YOUR LIFE, CHANGE THE WORLD
A Spiritual Guide to Living Now

*For a complete list of books, visit **okawabooks.com**.*